SMALL TALK, BIG NAMES

18 December 1993 —

To: AKIKO —

THE BEST ROADIE IN THE WORLD!

CONGRATULATIONS & GOOD LUCK. —

John O'Connell
Richmond College

SMALL TALK, BIG NAMES

40 Years of Rock Quotes

MYLES PALMER

MAINSTREAM
PUBLISHING

EDINBURGH AND LONDON

For Doug D'Arcy
and Danny Wright
– thanks for the Seventies, the Eighties
and, especially, the laughs.

The moral right of the author has been asserted

First published in Great Britain in 1993 by
MAINSTEAM PUBLISHING COMPANY (EDINBURGH) LTD
7 Albany Street
Edinburgh EH1 3UG

ISBN 1 85158 573 7

A catalogue record for this book is available from the British Library

Typeset in Baskerville No. 2 by Litho Link Limited, Welshpool, Powys, Wales

Printed in Great Britain by The Cromwell Press, Melksham

Contents

Preface

The best time to do a book of rock quotes is when there is nothing much happening in music, and that makes 1993 an ideal moment to compile a history of rock music in other people's words. A quotes book, by definition, is retro, a compilation by Various Artists.

Rock has no guitarists as quotable as Oscar Wilde, and no songstresses as witty as Dorothy Parker, but it has its moments. In January 1993 I read in *The Mail On Sunday* that former Rolling Stones manager Andrew Oldham had been interviewed recently on an American TV chat show. Asked how they could get The Beatles back together again, he said, 'Three more bullets!'

Some editors might feel compelled to explain why they have structured their book in a certain way, and say why they have emphasised this and ignored that, but instead of starting with an apology I'll just say a few words about where I'm coming from. I have tried, where possible in such a varied and contradictory mass of comments, to emphasise connections, influences and turning points, and to remember that men often reached for the sky by standing on the shoulders of the men who had gone before. Also, since this is not a review of the school play, I have not felt obliged to mention everybody.

This book, despite a lot of material about Elvis, The Beatles and Madonna, is a book whose heart lies in the Seventies.

It is only now, after researching the last four decades of popular music, that I have realised just how much happened in the Seventies, a period which is historically distant but still emotionally close, since it was the time which defined my attitude to the music business. The life you have as a bachelor who lives musician's hours (doing five gigs a week, and sometimes three in one night, and getting up at noon) is rather more varied than the life you have as a parent who bashes away on a word-processor from nine a.m. to seven p.m. every day.

It is also, I've realised, a rock critic's book. I didn't know many rock critics then, and know even fewer now, but I couldn't help noticing that when I got on a plane the journalist sitting next to me would often be carrying *Zigzag*, *Rolling Stone* and *Let It Rock*, doing his homework. I went to Glasgow once with Craig Copetas, an American who said *Rolling Stone* treated writers so badly that it would be the first magazine ever burned to the ground by its own staff. I didn't know about that, but in one story I did for them about Dutch band Focus they changed my copy to say that Holland was in Scandinavia. I never knew whether it was the drugs or the educational system.

When I started this book I wondered if any musicians had ever said anything significant or memorable to me. Unfortunately, a lot of it was a long time ago, and I've forgotten everything except a handful of situations and remarks. Some of them are so personal I don't know whether they would mean anything to anybody else, but here goes.

In 1965, when I was a student at Manchester University, I talked to The Beach Boys backstage at the Odeon Manchester in a week when *Good Vibrations* was Number One, and wrote a piece about it for the student newspaper almost as an afterthought, as a way of putting the night behind me. Even then, writing was forgetting.

I remember talking to Mike Love and stylish publicist Derek Taylor. Two 18-year-old girls stood beside us. One said, 'You write that column in *Disc*, don't you?' Derek admitted he did. 'And you always mention The Beach Boys, don't you?' Derek said, 'Yes, isn't that a coincidence!'

Derek later worked for Warner Brothers and I had some high times with him in London and New York. A man with genius for flattery, he once gave me a droll, dreamy autobiographical book he'd written, and I would certainly have used some quotes from that here if I had not foolishly lent it to someone.

I didn't know it in 1965, but I had already made my biggest mistake: I started at the top, which made me complacent. I made another huge mistake eight years later when Rod Stewart suggested that I write a book about The Faces. Having already written about them several times, I didn't want to write it all again at greater length, and it was not until 1979, when I was writing a book about Woody Allen, that I remembered Rod and realised that I should have jumped at the chance.

At the time Rod was the world's number one 'progressive' singer, and it would have been worthwhile to capture the great star and his merry men while the music and the atmosphere were still good, before it all collapsed into caricature and recriminations. Ten years down the line, when Susan Hill of Sidgwick's asked me to write an unauthorised biography of Mark Knopfler, I decided to do it just to punish myself for not writing The Faces book.

I was turned on to The Grateful Dead by Ian Pollock, *Time Out*'s first music editor, a benevolent rebel who, like Derek Taylor, loved to see his friends enjoying themselves, especially at his spacious flat in Willesden, where we used to roll around the floor giggling until it started to get light.

One afternoon in May 1972 I was standing on the stage with Jerry Garcia during a Dead soundcheck at Wembley Pool. He was showing me a guitar given to him by Graham Nash when promoter John Morris came in and tested the security barriers below the stage. He asked Garcia if they were okay. Uncle Jerry, the ultimate benign hippie, said, 'We don't need barriers, man – nobody's gonna attack us!'

Ian Pollock's nickname was Pol, and he pretty much disapproved of everything that was flash, arrogant, sexist, aggressive and satanic in The Rolling Stones. One day in 1974, after some particularly fine music on a sublime sunny afternoon at Knebworth, I said, 'You'd think some of The Stones would have come out to watch the Allman Brothers and Van Morrison, wouldn't you?' Pol's eyes twinkled as he said, 'Maybe they wouldn't dig the good vibes!' It was a very unkind thing to say, and untypical of Pol, but it made me laugh.

One day around that time I was with Van Morrison in a Chinese restaurant in Fulham and at a rehearsal studio nearby. He was wearing a crimson velvet jacket, and played some rather reflective, soulful piano. In a moment of over-enthusiasm, I heard myself say, 'I know people who'd give their life savings to see you in a club.' Van, smiling, said, 'How much are their life savings?'

Island Records pressman Brian Blevins phoned once and asked, 'Would you like to review Traffic in Munich?' I said, 'Sure, who else is going?' and he said, 'Just you.' So I flew over with Tom Hayes, their international guy. Also on the bill were Sutherland Brothers & Quiver, with whom I'd spent a week when they had an American hit and were supporting Elton John at Madison Square Garden, Nassau Coliseum and the Boston Gardens.

We had been warned that Germans are only into superstars, heavy metal and spacy electronics, and this proved to be the case. During SB&Q's set of sparkling pop-rock the crowd started to get restless, and eventually began whistles of derision. The band carried on playing, but after ten minutes Gavin Sutherland got pissed off and said, in English, 'Stop whistling at the back, it's bad manners!' Bass player Bruce Thomas added, 'And not only that, it's bad whistling!'

As usual I enjoyed Traffic's spacy, funky jamming with new man Rosko Gee on bass and the remarkable Reebop on percussion. Afterwards I bumped into Island boss Chris Blackwell, and we strolled backstage. He opened the dressing-room door and we walked in to find Steve Winwood and Jim Capaldi screaming at each other so fiercely that I wondered whether punches might be thrown. Chris smoothly escorted me back into the hallway. How embarrassing! Even Traffic wasn't all peace, love and joy.

Around that time I asked Blackwell about something I had been wondering about for two years. In 1971 I was at Morgan Studios with Rod Stewart while he was finishing off *Every Picture Tells A Story*, and we gave him the cover of *Time Out* just before *Maggie May*, when nobody knew who he was. In the studio toilet somebody had written, 'Chris Blackwell said *Whiter Shade of Pale* wouldn't be a hit.' When I mentioned this, Chris just said, 'I liked it, but I didn't think anybody else would like it.'

When I was with SB&Q in America we had three days off in Cambridge, Massachusetts, and one night we watched Airto and Fingers with Flora Purim in a club, and drank so many tequila sunrises that I wondered: was the music really that magical, or was it just the booze? I went back the next night and watched them straight and got just as high.

At one point four of us were in a pizza joint where the only other customers were two lovely, giggly college girls with newly washed hair and beautiful teeth. They were stealing glances from a booth across the aisle, so I told them to come over and join us.

We chatted for a while, amusing them with our gossip and boasting, and it was then that I realised American girls are different. Looking around at four long-haired Englishmen, the brunette made a remark which I found astonishing. She said, 'I'd like to ball all of you, but I only love one of you.' As it turned out, she didn't ball any of us, and we never knew which one she loved, but it is one of my favourite rock quotes because she said it in such a friendly and innocent way.

Trips to America usually produced one good line. On my first jaunt to New York in 1972 we were in a big black limousine whizzing up some freeway towards Alice Cooper's mansion in Greenwich, Connecticut, when I looked out the window towards Manhattan and saw several colossal skyscrapers. I said, 'Which one's the Empire State?' Alice said, 'It's the one with the gorilla on it!'

After playing The Rainbow in January 1974, Stevie Wonder mixed the concert highlights for Radio Luxembourg at Island studios, where he worked with my pal Brian Humphries, Traffic's engineer, and I spent two nights with them. Capital DJ Nicky Horne and singer Linda Lewis were there for a while, On the second night, Pete Townshend kept phoning up. He wanted Stevie to come over to his studio and put some clarinet on *Pinball Wizard* which he was re-recording for the soundtrack of Ken Russell's *Tommy*.

After a while Townshend arrived with Eric Clapton and Bob Pridden, The Who's soundman, carrying a bottle of brandy and a stack of paper cups in a cellophane wrapper, which I thought was sensible minimum apparatus for people who wanted to avoid interruptions to their drinking.

They sat outside, waiting and chatting among themselves, while Stevie, Brian, the tape operator and I were in the control room, so I went out and talked to them. Bob told me that once, when he was drunk, Pete admitted he had spent all night in a hotel corridor just so he could meet Georgie Fame. That didn't surprise me because I knew that musicians are the biggest groupies of all.

Eric recalled seeing Stevie at the Talk of the Town nightclub with a brilliant 16-year-old bass player who later joined Miles Davis. I assumed he knew that guitarist Marlo Henderson's wife had become ill in America, and that Marlo had flown home, missing the second pair of Rainbow shows. I said, 'If Stevie had phoned up and asked you to fill in for Marlo, would you have done it?' Clapton said, 'I'd have run all the way!' I had this vision of Eric sprinting down the motorway towards London carrying his guitar case in one hand. I'd love to have heard the most volcanic vocalist in rock pushed to new heights by the most inspired, soulful guitarist – my dream concert.

One of my golden rules is never to go backstage or to a party if I have not enjoyed the gig. I broke this rule only once, for Steely Dan at The Rainbow in 1974. They had two drummers, two bass players, two guitarists and two keyboard players, and they played too fast and too loud. I thought: typical American group, no confidence. But I went into the dressing-room and chatted to Donald Fagen, a New York hipster. The more I talked to him the more I liked him. So after a few minutes I said, 'I was here last week, and Traffic got a much bigger sound with four instruments than you got with eight.' Fagen said, 'Traffic is a far better band than us.' I admired him for admitting that, and I still play *The Royal Scam*.

In 1977 I knew Jill Furmanovsky, a photographer who blagged me into going to the Brecknock, a pub in Camden Town, to see Squeeze, who immediately became one of my favourite groups. Jill lived with Squeeze's manager Miles Copeland, who also handled The Police, his brother's band.

They had offices in Dryden Chambers, off Oxford Street, near the 100 Club, the Vortex and the Marquee. The building was a hive of punk activity, with Mark P. and Danny Baker producing *Sniffin' Glue*, the original fanzine, and many spikytops always hanging around, especially Sham 69, an endearing quartet of teenage louts led by gangling, big-hearted Jimmy Pursey. Malcolm McLaren's Glitterbest offices were on the floor above.

If I had noted down all the sub-literate slander and scatology which decorated the toilets at Dryden Chambers, it would have made a whole chapter of punk graffiti for this book, and provided fascinating source material for social historians.

One night Miles, Jill and I were sitting in the kitchen of Miles's house in Maida Vale, talking about groups. Miles was saying that as an agent and manager he tried to build each group up to the point where they were living on earnings rather than advances, so that then he could take on another band. 'But every new band you take on, the others hate you,' he moaned. I said, 'Sure, but life isn't a popularity contest. I wish I had ten pounds for everybody who's called me an arrogant bastard behind my back.' Jill smiled and said, 'Here's twenty quid!'

In 1992 I read *England's Dreaming*, The Sex Pistols book by Jon Savage, which is good, but too long, too political and too sociological for my own taste. I was surprised that Savage had not talked to my mate Stewart Joseph, co-manager of Generation X, the pretty-boy punk band that spawned Billy Idol. A few of Stewart's comments are included here, along with some interesting and hitherto unpublished comments made to me by bass player Rob Milne and record producer Pat Collier. Stewart, Pat and Rob are reliable eyewitnesses from the very earliest days and nights of the punk explosion, and can shed a lot more light on the phenomenon than people who were elsewhere at the time but who have since constructed vast pyramids of theory.

There were scores of exciting gigs in the Seventies, and lots of laughs, and I'd do it all again, even though I think you can have just as much fun doing a thousand other things.

One of the most memorable nights was Van Morrison and The Caledonian Soul Orchestra in 1973. I lived in Stroud Green, north London, a 15-minute walk from The Rainbow, where I knew the manager Ted Way and his assistant Peter Dally very well, so I went down to watch the soundcheck in the afternoon.

The ten musicians were tuning up and warming up. Then Van walked on and started to sing. I'll never forget the first impact of his voice coming through the PA as they cruised into *Here Comes the Night*. It was music of astounding power and beauty. Arriving again later, I met Richard Williams of *Melody Maker* who had been to Birmingham to see Van the night before. Richard said, 'It was the best thing I've ever seen in my life, and all I could think of was when can I see it again!'

I was thrilled by a unique concert, scribbled my review, and dashed into Ted's office to phone in 400 words to *The Times*. Then my girlfriend Jan (now Mrs Palmer) drove us down to Chelsea for the party at the White Elephant, a club on the river.

We were among the last to arrive. There was a vast spread of delicious-looking food, the most extravagant I had ever seen at a rock reception. Veteran liggers were so intimidated that they had formed a long, orderly queue. By this time I was starving and thought, 'Make way for the working press!' I barged to the front, grabbed a plate and piled it high with whatever I fancied. Nobody said anything.

We continued to mingle, chat and have a good time. An hour or two later I found myself standing next to a small, skinny, ugly-beautiful man from Dartford, the midnight rambler himself. I asked Mick Jagger how the album was going and he said, 'Finished it. We're thinkin' about the next one now.' I asked if he'd heard *Fresh*, the new Sly Stone album, and Mick said he'd been listening to it in the car on the way to the White Elephant. So I said, 'I love Sly, but he's really annoyed me because he's copped all Stevie Wonder's vocal mannerisms!' Mick said, 'Yeah, but everybody nicks from everybody else. Stevie Wonder copped all his piano licks from Billy Preston.'

A long time later I heard that Van had kept my review of The Rainbow concert in his wallet for years, and showed it to each new member of his band. I started to glow when I heard that, and I hope you'll glow a little bit when you read this collection of rock quotes. I've put some of my own favourites in the first chapter.

MYLES PALMER,
London,
March 1993

Favourites

Imagine six apartments
It isn't hard to do
One is full of fur coats
The other's full of shoes.
Elton John's 40th birthday card to John Lennon, 1980

Pop concerts are just gatherings of people who want to have a good time and I don't think they really have a higher meaning.
Mick Jagger, 1968

His overwriting was the equivalent in folk music of the happy energy of The Beatles. He loved language enough to misuse it.
Robert Christgau on Bob Dylan, Cheetah, *1967*

That Shakespeare was really somethin'. I wonder what he would have thought of my records?
Jerry Lee Lewis after playing Iago in 1966 rock musical Catch My Soul

Celebrity fucks people up. Celebrity knocks the stuffing out of people, personally and creatively. There's not much that fucks you up faster than celebrity and isolation.
George Michael, Bare, *1988*

How can you regret anything? I've had such a marvellous life. The last 20 years have been absolutely marvellous. If it all ended tomorrow I'd say it had been fabulous. I'd recommend this lifestyle to anybody!
Rod Stewart, 1986

When Marc Bolan made *Ride A White Swan*, he similarly stumbled upon a new and previously unrecognized teenage audience: upon a third distinct rock'n'roll generation – all ready to set up their own new heroes.
Andrew Weiner, New Society, *1972*

I'd like to create a new archetype, of someone who's in control of what he's doing.
Sting

You can't tell where the booing's going to come up. Can't tell at all. It comes up in the weirdest, strangest places and when it comes it's quite a thing in itself. I figure there's a little 'boo' in all of us.
Bob Dylan *press conference, 1965*

I feel like an actor when I'm onstage, not a rock artist. It's not much of a vocation, being a rock'n'roller.
David Bowie

What attracts me even more to The Band, Sly Stone, Randy Newman, and Elvis, is that these men tend to see themselves as symbolic Americans.
Greil Marcus, Mystery Train, *1977*

Well, compared to Elvis, The Stones were an entirely different class: they were as far ahead of him as Elvis himself had been ahead of the young Sinatra.
Nik Cohn, *1968*

The key to building a superstar is to keep their mouth shut. To reveal an artist to the people can be to destroy him. It isn't to anyone's advantage to see the truth. In the long run the audience matters more.
Bob Ezrin, *record producer*

A star, so legend goes, is a person possessed of charisma, of an aura of the extraordinary. A person, moreover, in touch with strange and mysterious forces. And it's true that a star does possess charisma, that he *is* in touch with such forces. But charisma is hardly innate, and those forces are mysterious only to the extent that we refuse to examine them.
Andrew Weiner, New Society, *1973*

I saw Queen. It was an all-right show, but I had 2nd row tickets & was forced to look at Brian May's legs for nearly two hours straight. Brian May has the ugliest damn legs I have ever seen. They look like dog arms with shoes on the paws. I love your mag.
Letter to Creem *from Houston, Texas, June 1978*

I don't know why I bother, really, because people don't listen to lyrics in rock'n'roll records too much.
Lou Reed, *1989*

We've put out good records for *years*. That's the main thing, that's what a lot of other bands haven't done. We've lasted because of the songs.
Mick Jagger, *1976*

To the outside adult eye, Punk Rock is the weirdest, ugliest, nastiest, scariest, most thoroughly repulsive and flat-out *incomprehensible* variant on the Teenage Wasteland formula that they've ever seen.
Charles Shaar Murray, *1977*

When Dylan is inspired, he sings as though every lyrical and rhythmic and melodic phrase in a song is subdivided into thousands of parts, and he can intuitively move among those parts, emphasizing, extending, combining, holding back, shaping each moment of the song as he sings it.
Paul Williams, Bob Dylan, Performing Artist, *1990*

As they were so into The Faces, they'd go down to Richmond, to Sir John Mills's old house, which Ron Wood had just bought. Keith Richards used to stay in the little cottage at the bottom of Ron's garden. Steve and others would get in there, rifle around it, have a go on one of Keith's guitars, nick a shirt and leave a little note saying 'Steve was here'. That was their fun of a Saturday night.
Glen Matlock, I Was A Teenage Sex Pistol, *1990*

At present we have a society based on having and owning; we need a society based around being and giving.
Mike Scott, *The Waterboys*

In the space of two years Alice Cooper has lived the whole rise and plummet trip and then some. Starting with *Love It To Death*, they gave us one classic, *Eighteen*, and a couple other good tunes. *Killer* was mostly terrific but cluttered up with two long death-gadget numbers. They made up for it by putting on the most exciting R & R shows around at the time . . . Who needs music when you're out for fucks, bucks and laughs?
Fusion *magazine*, *1973, on* Billion Dollar Babies

I make the record. I give it to the record company and it's in the grooves. You know what I mean. No matter what anybody writes, no matter what ego trips people are on . . . the music is there.
Van Morrison, *1973*

There were three toilets for half a million people. They were selling them aspirin to get them stoned. For ten miles along the freeway there were abandoned cars. There were cars turned over in the river. It was like someone had said, 'You've got ten seconds to get out of the city before it's destroyed.'
Ozzie Osbourne *after the Indiana Soda Pop Festival, 1972*

Christ, I wish I had someone to share all this with.
Elton John, *1976*

Most bands don't make money. They just squander it on producers and cocaine and lots of other bullshit, and it's disgusting. There's so much idiotic excess. It goes beyond enjoyment.
Sting

I'm as stupid as the next person.
Van Morrison, *1989*

Messages become a drag, like preaching. I think one of the worst possible beliefs is that pop stars know any more about life than anyone else.
Nick Mason, *Pink Floyd*

To sell a million in this country you have to get to the young marrieds.
Jonathan Morrish, *CBS Records*

The next few years are going to make great demands on Rod Stewart, and I think he intends to get through without a mark on him, like the kid in *Every Picture Tells A Story*: move out and get the lay of the land, dodge the cops, never let the good slip away, make friends and learn how to keep them, come back older, a little wiser, still free, but with a better idea of what freedom means – and don't let the bastards get ya. Rod Stewart is the best we've got, and I hope he makes it.
Greil Marcus, Creem, *1972*

A curmudgeonly old bugger? So they say. But for the enchanting beauty of his music, you'd forgive him anything.
Paul Du Noyer, Q, *1988, on Van Morrison*

A huge insecurity is obviously the motivating force for most artists. And I understand that. But I feel that it's dangerous on a personal level to have a huge gap between what you are in your work and what you are in reality.
George Michael

It is an iron law of pop music that if you go away for too long, you come back sounding like the people who've ripped you off in the interim. This sad fate has befallen the great, original New York art-rockers Television, who returned to the Town and Country Club 14 years after they first split up sounding too much like Lloyd Cole for comfort.
Ben Thompson, Independent on Sunday, *1992*

In the Eighties we have to say that rock'n'roll went to work for the corporation, and got up at six o'clock in the morning. And it wasn't just to keep fit. It was to get ahead; to improve the prospects of the corporation.
Bono, *1988*

The attribution of 'magical' qualities to particular individuals can be viewed, in one way, as a regression to childhood. It implies the same inability, or refusal, to distinguish reality from unreality.
Andrew Weiner, New Society, *1973*

Sweat is to Springsteen what make-up is to Boy George.
The Independent, *1988*

Rock never managed to die before it got old. Instead, it put on a bit of weight and became part of a giant showbusiness mainstream. It now offers a fairly secure career to artists with tenacity, a thick skin and sound business management. The Russians are probably the only people left on the planet who regard popular music as 'subversive'.
Adam Sweeting, The Guardian, *1986*

By MTV trying to visualise the music they automatically stripped it of most of its natural mystery and depth. Before rock video, when people were confronted with the music, they had to rely on their own natural ability to utilise their imagination.
Neil Young, *1990*

Just imagine our pop culture, had it presented nothing but positive images – Lou Reed singing about heroism not heroin; a sober Jim Morrison screaming, 'Mother I want to . . . wish you happy birthday!' Those who demand that popular culture present positive images seek to claim the moral high ground; but the allure of popular culture has always been its promise of a walk on the wild side.
Cosmo Landesman, The Guardian, *1993*

SMALL TALK, BIG NAMES

I got a letter inviting me to a ceremony in L.A. where they put a star for him in Hollywood Boulevard. That would have been about the biggest insult imaginable in the Sixties, to suggest to him that one day, Jimi, you will be such a part of the establishment, they will put a star for you on Hollywood Boulevard. It was as if everything he had stood against and played against was being forced upon him after he'd died.
Gerry Stickells, *Hendrix's original road manager*

When we got to the Manhattan Club, Muddy preceded Johnny, Ebby and myself up to the box office and announced, 'I'm Muddy Waters.' The cashier said, 'A dollar fifty.' Muddy just reached in his pocket and forked it out with no comment. From that experience I swore never to announce myself in hopes of getting anything gratis, regardless of what height I might rise to in fame.
Chuck Berry, The Autobiography, *1987*

Sex

Being a rock star is like having a sex change. People stare at you, follow you down the street shouting comments, they hustle you and touch you up. I now know what it must feel like to be a woman.
U2's **Bono**, *1992*

Folksingers get laid a lot more than the other kids in high school. Even if you have to do it in the afternoon on the floor of the coffeehouse.
David Crosby, *1974*

You were at school and you were pimply and no one wanted to know you. You get into a group and you've got thousands of chicks there. And there you are with thousands of little girls screaming their heads off. Man, it's power – phew!
Eric Clapton

From the start there were a lot of ladies, and that escalated.
Noel Redding, *Jimi Hendrix Experience*

Looks are like honey to a degree. They'll attract flies, bees, bears. They don't necessarily keep them.
Terence Trent D'Arby, *1987*

The last time I was in L.A. there was this incredible groupie feud which was getting down to razor-blade sandwiches. The competition thing out there is incredible.
Jimmy Page, *1975*

I think it's very healthy – you can't overdose on ladies. You can shoot stuff until you're dead, but you can't make love until you're dead, your body just doesn't work any more.
Bill Wyman

I hate, more than anything, sexless music.
Michael Hutchence, *INXS*

I'm sexy. How can I avoid it? I'd have to put a bag over my head. But then my voice would come across. And it's sexy.
Madonna

I'm not a sex symbol. I'll leave that to Madonna.
Belinda Carlisle

As for sexism, well, I *hate* women. Why do I even have to have a reason for that?
Iggy Pop, *1979*

I love fucking. My appetite is as healthy as it could possibly be for a normal, red-blooded 27-year-old man.
Terence Trent D'Arby, *1989*

I think what someone should point out that what they're doing is ignorant and naive. They're telling people that it's naughty to be gay. But this is 1984 and we should be educating people in another way. Frankie aren't saying to people, how can we enlighten you? It's saying, 'Look – ha, ha, ha – isn't it disgusting?' That really disgusted me. They've put things back 20 years.
Boy George *in a letter to* Record Mirror

I tell you all the bitches – all the women – want me now because they can sense that strength in me, and they want it *so* bad. But they're not gonna get me. Only on my own terms, and my terms are simply phoning 'em up, telling them to be at such and such a place at such and such a time, in good physical condition, to be fucked and then leave, goddammit.
Iggy Pop, *1979*

If I was gay I swear I would say it but I ain't never liked a woman in my bed, I swear to God. And Robyn is my friend. I've known her since high school. She's my good friend. But no, I ain't gay and never have been gay.
Whitney Houston, *1992*

In this town there's four sexes – men, women, homosexuals and Girl Singers.
Judy Henske, *folk singer, to Linda Ronstadt in* Q, *1990*

You never really know a guy until you ask him to wear a rubber.
Madonna *to crowd at Wembley Stadium, 1990*

Best kept secret in the music business? That George Michael is a heterosexual.
Boy George, *1989*

I'm not a big fan of Tracy Chapman but it's about time that a black woman is allowed to come across without having to wear a leather skirt where you can see her pubic hair sticking out.
Terence Trent D'Arby, *1989*

Jimmy Page represented all that was ethereal, exquisite, divine, and pornographic in rock music for me.
Pamela Des Barres, *supergroupie, 1989*

I have constant battles with people to stop them sending big, flashy cars to pick me up. They think I want to ride around in a big penis.
Sinead O'Connor, *1990*

He sure left his mark, that cat. I know of five kids, at least. All by different chicks, and they all look like Brian.
Keith Richards *on Brian Jones*

I thought everybody in rock had illegitimate children.
Rod Stewart

As far as I'm concerned, the benefit of being a black Irishman is that I pull more chicks.
Phil Lynott, *Thin Lizzy*

David Bowie is a little too fairyish for me. I guess it's because I'm American, but I don't like to see boys wearing make-up.
Patti Smith

Sometimes an orgasm is better than being on stage. Sometimes being on stage is better than an orgasm.
Mick Jagger

I think Mick Jagger would be astounded and amazed if he realised to how many people he is *not* a sex symbol.
Angie Bowie

I don't want to be known as a fag. I want to be known as a singer.
Tom Robinson

SMALL TALK, BIG NAMES

By the time it was over, he had lapped and nuzzled his guitar with his lips and tongue, caressed it with his inner thighs, jabbed at it with a series of powerful pelvic thrusts. Even the little girls who'd come to see The Monkees understood what this was about.
Lillian Roxon on Jimi Hendrix at Monterey, 1967

I only remember a city by its chicks.
Jimi Hendrix

I am the back door man. The men don't know, but the little girls understand.
Jim Morrison

For many of the girls, it's the first time their little thighs get twitchy.
David Cassidy's road manager

You look for certain things in certain towns. Chicago, for instance, is notorious for two things at once. Balling two chicks, or three, in combination acts.
Jimmy Page

We're not opposed to stage flash – we just don't want to look like a bunch of faggots.
J. Geils

On stage, I make love to 25,000 different people, then I go home alone.
Janis Joplin

A lot of tunes in the guise of romanticism have mainly fucking behind them.
Randy Newman

The great thing about being 30 is that there are a great deal more available women. The young ones look younger and the old ones don't look nearly as old.
Glenn Frey, The Eagles

I'm saving the bass player for Omaha.
Janis Joplin

I knew Richard was gay and asked him right out if he was referring to only him and me having a party. He said, 'Chuck, I've always wanted to perform with you since the first time I saw you on television and have thought about it ever since.'
Chuck Berry *on Little Richard*

Maybe if the audience can see a cock through a pair of trousers, that must make you a sex symbol.
Robert Plant

I'm pretty much over my affection for men. The only time I get halfway wistful for those old days is in Japan. All those little boys are so cute. I just want to take them *all* up to my room.
David Bowie

I just wanna fuck my mother, basically. Always have done. Not so much now, because she's getting a bit older. She's losing her grip on her looks. She's a cute little French girl.
Jean-Jacques Burnel, *The Stranglers*

On that first tour of America there was a point where George was fucking everything that moved, from air hostesses to unbelievable amounts of girls . . . Halfway through that tour he thought, hold on a minute. I'm getting what I want but at the end of the day they're sleeping with *George Michael*. He didn't like being used like that. I'm talking about three or four girls a *night*. It was serious. But Andrew never stopped. He would still fuck anything. It was different for the two of them. Andrew doesn't mind people using him. George does.
Andros Georgiou, *friend of George Michael*, Bare, *1988*

Drugs

When I carried a gun it was paranoia. Cocaine paranoia. You think everybody is after you and when Lennon got blown away I used that as a dumb excuse to carry a gun. I needed some rationalisation for packing a piece all the time so I used that.
David Crosby, 1981

I've got no time for drugs any more. I tried them all and wouldn't recommend any of them.
Mick Jagger

I don't take drugs. I've seen great musicians become nothing but snivelling, diseased mongrels because of drugs.
Ted Nugent

I'm extremely careful. I've never turned blue in someone else's bathroom. I consider that the height of bad manners.
Keith Richards

I'm glad they didn't have drugs in the Sixties when I was in high school, because if they'd had drugs, I'd still be in high school.
Joe Walsh

I felt in retrospect that getting rid of the drugs allowed the real problems to surface. It allowed light to come into a lot of dark corners, and then you had to deal with the real issues that the drugs had just been covering up. That's a process of several years.
Rosanne Cash, 1990

Back in the early Sixties, before San Francisco first uttered the word *psychedelic*, Jerry Lee and his band, The Memphis Beat, were arrested at a motel in Grand Prairie, Texas, and charged with possession of seven hundred amphetamine capsules; two hundred were for the band, five hundred for Jerry Lee.
Nick Tosches, Country, *1985*

Johnny Cash was arrested in El Paso in 1964 for 'smuggling and concealing' 688 Dexedrine capsules and 475 Equanil tablets. 'I'd talk to the demons,' Cash said in 1975, 'and they'd talk back to me – and I could *hear* them. I mean, they'd say, "Go on, John, take twenty more milligrams of Dexedrine, you'll be all right".'
Nick Tosches, Country, *1985*

In extreme cases marijuana can so destroy a man's character that he mixes freely with persons of another race.
South African criminology textbook, 1966

Hippies in England represent about as powerful a challenge to the power structure of the state as people who put foreign coins in their gas meters.
David Widgery

I had taken some strong psychedelics right before I went on stage. I was struggling to keep myself grounded. My guitar was like rubber.
Carlos Santana *on Woodstock*

The strange thing to me was that I never really knew how much dope they were putting down their throats. Jimi never seemed to be high. I didn't know he had taken acid and this was the guy who shared the same flat with me. You couldn't tell with Jimi. It never showed. He just cruised through everything.
Chas Chandler

The greatest thing I discovered at university was marijuana.
Hugh Cornwell, *The Stranglers*

Magic is doin' it so well that you get it up beyond mechanical levels. Magic is making people feel good and stuff. Magic is, if you're high on psychedelics, having a great big love beast crawl out of your amplifiers and eat the audience.
David Crosby, *1970*

One of the problems was I got off the pills. I couldn't stand it. Once I got off it, I realised how much the band had deteriorated through playing on speed. And that made it really hard. And I just worked from then on to get everybody else off it.
Roger Daltrey, *1975*

It never gave me brain damage or anything at all like that. I shouldn't really own up to it even now. I took it before it was made illegal.
Mick Jagger, *1974, on acid*

I was late trying everything. I was so over-protected within this stable. When Crosby, Stills, Nash and Young did their first album all I knew was suddenly all their personalities were changing. Graham was getting thin. He wouldn't eat and he stayed up all night. I didn't know any of them was doing drugs. They would hide them and whisper when I was around.
Joni Mitchell, *1988*

I did some good writing, I think, on cocaine – *Song For Sharon* – but it kills your heart, takes all your energy, puts it up in your brain and gives you the arrogance that, you know, ruined Jaco Pastorius. I watched it ruin a lot of people.
Joni Mitchell, *1988*

I hate seeing people who are high on drugs at my concerts. It makes my blood boil. It's particularly bad in Germany where you can smell the marijuana before you get on stage. Drugs are such a stupid waste of time.
Phil Collins

I got registered as an addict, which is really the first step to getting out. Because the first thing you have to do is admit you're on the stuff, which you tend not to do. I spent at least three years pretending I wasn't a junkie, that I didn't really 'need' heroin. Which is nonsense. And when you have to go to a clinic every day to pick it up, along with all the other junkies, then you know.
Marianne Faithfull, *1978*

I can watch people die. I've seen people croak and I've thrown them out the window . . . out the window because you don't want the body in the pad. You might get busted anyway for what you're doing already.
Tim Hardin, *singer-songwriter, 1972*

I spend all my money on drugs for other people. I want people to take drugs – it's better than playing Monopoly.
Lou Reed *to reporters at Sydney airport, Australia, 1974*

He said there was never a day in his life when he didn't have to have something. I would say that there was never a day in which he didn't

have to have two or three different drugs. Because John was your classic multiple-drug abuser. I mean, he was an alcoholic. He was an addict. He smoked marijuana the way an ordinary smoker smoked cigarettes. He became a junkie at 26, and he remained a junkie, if we include methadone.
Albert Goldman on John Lennon, 1988

I'm here to tell you drugs are important in a person's life. Someone who's doing a lot of drugs, they're not the same person any more.
Albert Goldman, 1988

The dole is a venerable socialist institution, we've all been on it. Money for drugs – don't knock it.
John Perry, The Only Ones

It's hard to come to terms with. You hate yourself so much for just being an idiot. Y'know, when people say, 'What've you been doing for the past seven or eight years?' and you say, 'Sitting in a room, taking drugs', it doesn't sound very constructive.
Peter Perrett, The Only Ones, 1989

The public hungers to see talented young people kill themselves.
Paul Simon

I think music is magic. I think it's always been mankind's party, but I think what happens is there are peripheral things – chicks, glory, money, fame . . . I've been very fortunate in that I was exposed to those things very early on, and the only one that ever really derailed me was drugs. I managed not to take the rest of it too seriously, particularly fame and stardom. I don't see them as being real.
David Crosby, 1989

My mind still seems to work, I can remember phone numbers. I seem able to string sentences together. I'm amazed, frankly, because I took it as far as you can go and still be alive, and I almost wasn't a couple of times.
David Crosby, 1989

That scene all changed in the Eighties, didn't it? It went from a harmless jazz Woodbine to people getting destroyed with cocaine. We never got involved with cocaine.
Gary Brooker, Procol Harum, 1992

I'm the one that's got to die when it's time for me to die, so let me live my life the way I want to.
Jimi Hendrix

During Zeppelin's heyday in the Seventies, when Plant was by his own admission 'a silly little boy with some powder up me nose', World War V or the landscape of Mars could have gone past outside the windows without anybody noticing, such was the revved-up tunnel vision of this legendary unit.
Adam Sweeting

I get asked a lot about drugs. I sometimes feel I get more respect for not being a heroin addict than for anything I've done musically. That pisses me off. I feel like saying, 'Hold on a second, honey, do you know how much money I've brought into this country?'
Boy George, 1989

All I can say is that drugs are a retreat. Artistic people are by nature so volatile, and if you're highly strung, which I am, you are vulnerable.
Boy George, 1989

I never followed the Boy George story in terms of worrying where Ecstasy was leading me – I could see the vast differences between his character and mine . . . I've always been very good at stopping things. At the end of the day I'm a very moderate character, which is one of the reasons I find it easier to survive than other people.
George Michael, Bare, *1988*

It's become a bit of a pain. I don't think the band drink any more or less than most bands. But we have this image that was created for us, we didn't make it ourselves. There's no way, if we were as pissed as newts every night, that we'd be able to play the way we do.
Terry Woods, The Pogues, 1989

For somebody who burnt the candle at both ends, Shane's doing pretty well to be still around. He's never really made a go of cleaning himself up, let's hope he does soon. He's been on holiday in Greece, and is looking a lot healthier.
Darryl Hunt, The Pogues, 1991

The surprising thing about heroin is that you believe you can make yourself invisible. The minute your eyelids begin to droop, there is no one else in the room.
Eric Clapton, 1985

It was a typical junkie scene. It was despicable.
Pete Townshend on Clapton and Alice Ormsby-Gore, 1971–72

I was having to answer hysterical phone calls from Alice practically every night. She always wanted me to go over there. It was an hour and a half's drive, and always at awkward hours of the night.
Pete Townshend

For years Eric and Alice had opened none of the mail arriving at the house. When Pattie moved in in 1974, she discovered 'mail everywhere, with lots of brown envelopes containing about £5,000 in out-of-date cheques'.
Ray Coleman, 1985

In the case of heroin, the drug's failure for Eric was not to live up to his expectations in helping him create some work of genius, or help him towards some profound recognition of life.
Ray Coleman, 1985

When I came off drugs I was left with a huge vacuum, a huge hole, which I couldn't fill because at that time my belief in anything other than myself wasn't really very adequate. The only way I could fill it was with booze.
Eric Clapton

Fame

The very weird religion of celebrity scares me. It's like people are creating fake heroes because they don't have any real ones. The politicians have failed us, religion has failed us, so who do people turn to? Celebrities. It's wrong.
Michael Stipe, REM, 1992

All artists go through a period where they turn on success or success turns on them. Most of them can't ride that out. I guess I was fortunate in that I had been playing and singing for 13 years when success came. It touched me deeply but it didn't make me crazy.
Roy Orbison, 1988

It's not commonplace for people to get to the top of this profession when they're very young and then to live happily ever after.
George Michael

Fame threw me for a loop at first. I learned how to swim with it and turn it around. So you can just throw it in the closet and pick it up when you need it.
Bob Dylan

I don't mind signing autographs and I don't get tired of the fans either. It's natural to want to be liked, and I enjoy it. You can't remain in show business without being an extrovert.
Cliff Richard, 1971

I need to feel easy about myself, to lead a proper existence; being a celebrity comes second. In moments of honesty, I'd say all I've ever wanted was to be liked by a lot of people.
Boy George, 1989

It's a frame of mind. Of *course* you can do things like going into a pub. The thing to do is just go in and have a drink. But if you walk in wearing a double-breasted mink jacket, obviously people treat you as something different.
Cliff Richard, 1971

George always gets pissed off when he meets someone more famous than he is.
Jon Moss, *Culture Club drummer*

Is there anything worse than a really bad photograph? A photograph can make any person look like a saint, an angel, a fool, a devil, a nonentity. A lot of it is chance and a lot of it is malice. And a lot of it is idolatry. A bad photograph can give you several moments of real psychic loss.
Jim Morrison, *1969*

Even before I was famous I never enjoyed being in a crowd. I feel . . . inferior. I would go to discos with friends and my only concern was, where's the exit? I feel better in a crowd if I have people protecting me. You can never be too sure who's out there, who loves you so much they hate you.
Whitney Houston, *1992*

I get worried about the scale of success. Because basically I'm a very private person and I don't get a thrill from seeing my picture in the paper. I used to when I was 19 but I don't now. I turn the page very quickly now. I want to make records and I want a lot of people to hear them, but I don't really want to be famous. I'm not Paul Young, I'm not Prince, and I'm not the Thompson Twins.
Mike Scott, *The Waterboys*

The first flush of fame is all a bit hazy. And I didn't know what I was doing then – not as a writer and certainly not as a performer. But I knew what I wanted and when I was likely to get it. And seeing your dreams come true gives you a certain confidence.
George Michael, Bare, *1988*

I don't pay any attention to that fame stuff. Where I'm from people don't let you act the rock star. It's very working-class and no one gives a shit.
Jon Bon Jovi, *1991*

People do assume that if you're engaged in this whirlwind that you are surrounded by friends, enormously rich, the world is at your fingertips, you have enormous ease and the pick of the crowd, which has never ever been true in my case, nor in the performers I personally know.
Morrissey, *1990*

There's a barrier that you see around people who have been in the business a long time. There's a barrier around them, even when they are smiling at you, and nobody gets through that barrier. It's an inability to relate to anyone or anything. And no matter how strong a personality you are, that happens to you if you stay in the business long enough.
George Michael

A biographer's primary responsibility is to deliver the life. Not extract all the possible meanings. Because he can't. A life is like a poem. It has infinite meaning. But what's troublesome is that people read this stuff and they don't try to draw any meaning out of it. I mean, my biographies, they certainly tell you a hell of a lot about *fame*.
Albert Goldman, *1988*

There are a staggering number of similarities between Lennon and Elvis. The two greatest men in the history of rock and roll, which is how I conceive of Elvis and Lennon, were both so much akin in their psychic essence. *They are both momma's boys.* They were very bluesy, melancholic, withdrawn people looking for powerful, dominating keepers to direct them and also protect them. Both drifting off into the world of drugs. Both taken up with fantasies of being Jesus, of coming back as the messiah, and all that. Very unfulfilled by their fame.
Albert Goldman, *1988*

Money

I give The Stones about another two years. I'm saving for the future. I bank all my song royalties, for a start.
Mick Jagger, 1964

You know you're poor when you have to make a fire and you ain't got no wood. I've seen people pull wood off their houses to make a fire in the house. That's poor. And I was one of the people pulling wood off the house.
Little Richard on early life in Macon, Georgia

This was my richest time, with all my hit records selling all over the country and me and my band working every night. The river was running. The river of loot.
Little Richard

At the height of my career our initial guarantee had risen to about $2,500 a night, plus 50 per cent of the take over double the guarantee amount. Most often we would walk out with maybe $10,000 or $15,000 as our part of the total gate receipt.
Little Richard

If I had the money that's been stolen from me, I could build a church the likes of which you'd never seen. They took everything but my clothes – and they would have stolen them if I hadn't been sleeping with my socks on! But I was having so much fun I didn't really know what was going on.
Little Richard

One time we were appearing on the same package as Richard in New Jersey – though much lower down the bill. The Famous Flames were stranded in New Jersey with no money to get us back to Georgia. We asked Richard for a loan. He opened the trunk of his car, reached in, and scooped out of a handful of dollars without even looking. The trunk of the car was *full* of loose notes of all denominations!
Bobby Brown, James Brown's keyboard player

When Mother saw the house she couldn't believe it. She had never seen black people living in this type of house. It was the kind of house that white film stars lived in – big staircase, chandeliers, marble floors, plants, bedrooms upstairs and downstairs, and statues. Really lavish.
Little Richard

They asked me to come back the next day and I said if they gave me ten bob I would. So they gave me the ten bob, and I came back.
Noel Redding auditions for the Jimi Hendrix Experience

Money? For sure. The first taste of it I got, man, I wanted it all. The best dope, the most expensive chicks, the most outrageous scene. I wanted houses and cars – just crap. It's all crap.
David Crosby, 1974

The management and the record company joined our own greed. You can't really blame them or us. There was a multimillion dollar time-bomb out there.
Steve Winwood on Blind Faith

The Byrds never made any fucking money. The biggest year I had with The Byrds was probably 50 grand. It was a five-way split with a bum record deal. We never made money on our records and, come to think of it, we never really were a performance draw either.
David Crosby, 1974

I'm still working-class, because I give most of my money away. If you really want to know, at this very moment, I've got an overdraft of £250,000.
Pete Townshend, 1979

That's one of the problems of rock'n'roll, when a kid of twenty-two or three gets successful and goes to a $200,000-a-year place in space and thinks, 'Shit, I can play the drums and earn $200,000 a year – fuck these guys!' And they go out on their own and they find out that it's all a mistake – ya know?
Lowell George, 1975

For one night in the States I earned more than my old man did in his entire working life.
Jim Capaldi, Traffic

If you don't go for as much money as you can possibly get, then I think you're stupid.
Mick Jagger

What's money? A man is a success if he gets up in the morning and gets to bed at night and in between he does what he wants to.
Bob Dylan

I have the ability to think like a thief.
Allen Klein, Beatles manager, 1972

In early '67, I found out we were earning £200 or £400 a night and we were still getting paid £25 a week.
Noel Redding, 1992

All I got from Malcolm McLaren was an initial $1,000, and $2,000 for being in the film. It was a great rock'n'roll swindle. I was swindled totally, right down the line.
Sex Pistol Ronnie Biggs, 1977

We had a chance – we could have gone for the money and done a million *Rich Girls* and been the Doobie Brothers Jr . . . It's the American way to go for the big bucks all the time. The old capitalist system is if you have something just keep on going for it – sell yourself out if you have a shot. We're not like that. We're not that kind of people.
Daryl Hall, 1980

In England everybody's trying to make money but they're ashamed to admit it. Here it's easy to talk business.
Jon Moss in New York, 1982

The biggest turn-on about having shitloads of money is the ability to do what you like. All that shite about being the biggest, the best, the loudest . . . it's all meaningless. What matters is that when you're mega you can afford an independence that a lot of those so-called indie bands can't.
Bono, 1992

We're no longer a nation of shopkeepers, we're a nation of cowboys. The whole country is geared up for the professional cowboy to take over – it's all part of the Eighties ethic of 'Grab what you can now at any cost'.
Kirsty MacColl, 1989

You'll never see me being sponsored by Pepsi Cola, Coke or Levis, because I have no price on my head. I can't be bought! My art is more important to me than just being remembered as the person who got five million to be sponsored by Coca Cola!
Terence Trent D'Arby, *1989*

I'm not living in a cave. Like with Honda, they got in touch with me to do a commercial and I thought: Well, Miles Davis did a Honda commercial, so if it's good enough for Miles, it's certainly good enough for me.
Lou Reed, *1989*

I never had polio, which is a frightening thing for a dancer to think about, but I knew God had tested me and my brothers and sisters in other ways – our large family, our tiny house, the small amount of money we had to make ends meet, even the jealous kids in the neighbourhood who threw rocks at our windows while we rehearsed, yelling that we'd never make it.
Michael Jackson *in* Moonwalk, *his autobiography*

I don't think you'll see another artist sell that many tickets ever again.
Frank DiLeo, *Michael Jackson's manager, after Jacko had drawn 794,000 people to 11 outdoor concerts in UK in 1988*

Ego

There's nobody in the world can make better records than I do.
Phil Spector

Everybody argues, then we do what I say.
Bono, *1987*

I'm not being big-headed, but The Kinks were unique – it's like getting to the North Pole first. Really, until we started diversifying, we couldn't be touched.
Ray Davies

Take it from guys who know. Joni Mitchell is about as modest as Mussolini.
David Crosby, *1974*

I don't mean to sound big-headed, but I honestly don't think we've put a foot wrong in 20 years.
Mike Rutherford, *Genesis, 1989*

I don't like the attitude of the people here by and large. People don't like fame or success. There's no respect shown.
Andrew Ridgeley, *1990*

When *Magical Mystery Tour* was finally finished, Paul screened it for everyone at NEMS. The reaction was unanimous: it was awful. It was formless, disconnected, disjointed, and amateurish. I told Paul to junk it. 'So what, we lost £40,000,' I said. 'Better to junk it than be embarrassed by it.' But Paul's ego wouldn't let him consider this.
Peter Brown, *1983*

I've been through it all. I've been a puppet, the arsehole, the dupe, the junkie, and I've come through it all and proved that I'm the equal of anybody you'd care to mention.
Iggy Pop, *1979*

I am a brilliant guitarist. I know I can blow any other guitarist that's around today off the stage.
Ritchie Blackmore *of Deep Purple, 1975*

For a start, the band is much more handsome since I joined.
Sid Vicious

I get pretty terrified, to be honest, when I'm on tour. You really have to muster a lot of ego, to go out there, which I find rather draining.
Michael Hutchence, *INXS, 1990*

I'm egotistical about my *So It Goes/What's On* period. I put 42 bands on TV and I was right about every one of them. And there were 327 bands not on . . . and I was right about all of them as well! And I'll be on top form again when Northside are a monstrous group. If not, I'm an idiot. But we'll see.
Tony Wilson, *Factory Records founder*, NME, *1991*

Among the reasons given for the company's failure was Factory's approach to contracts with its bands: put simply, until the last year or so, it didn't have any. Almost all of Factory's bands did not have contracts. When London Records wanted to find out what the agreement was between Factory and New Order they were told there was no contract. Then a Factory employee remembered there was one piece of paper. He found it: the document said that New Order owned their own music.
Jay Rayner, Select, *1993*

Factory was also accused of being too kind to its artists, giving them way above the usual royalty.
Jay Rayner

It was crazy to behave like this. Tony always said that it was the bands that mattered, but they were taking him for a ride.
A former Factory band manager

I've always said from the very beginning that I'm going to do something to change music. I've always thought that music the way it is isn't all there is – there has to be more. There has to be something besides the scale. That's the burning obsession in my life. I don't know if I'm close, or what. If I can ever unlock the secrets, unlock a whole new musical world for people. Set a whole new scale, a whole new

dimension outside of what we know now. I think that would be fantastic.
Marvin Gaye, 1973

I think I'm right on the threshold of bursting through. I feel I'm as good as Beethoven or any of the greats. I don't compare myself to Beethoven, I must make that clear. I just think that I'm capable of all that he was capable of.
Marvin Gaye, 1973

I don't think people mind if I'm conceited. Every rock'n'roll star in the world is conceited.
Mick Jagger

I'll lay a £100,000 bet with anyone, any journalist, that there'll be a point in my career when I win an Oscar in Hollywood. There's no doubt about it.
Wendy James, Transvision Vamp, 1991

Quick success makes people very obnoxious and very unappreciative. We became a pair of incredibly obnoxious people.
Marc Almond on Soft Cell, 1990

I try to bring back some intelligence to music, instead of just four chords and dumb lyrics. I'll match the power of my ballads with anything Nirvana are doing.
Barry Manilow

If I'm just a footnote to Springsteen, that's okay with me.
John Mellencamp

Just because you're successful, doesn't make you any wiser.
The Edge, U2, 1988

We know what we are. What we have in this band is very special. The sound may be classical in one sense, but it's naturally our own. We don't sound like any other group. Our songs are different – they hold emotions of a spiritual nature.
Bono, 1982

Sometimes I feel that the only friends performers can have are other performers, but then there's that strange jealousy, that strange air of

competition that creeps in. I've never felt it because I've always been happy with my status – it's very respectable and useful.
Morrissey, *1990*

I saw Michael Jackson in an indoor arena in America, and it wasn't great. When I see something like that I think: My God, put *me* in charge for a week and I'll turn this into something good!
Dave Gilmour, *Pink Floyd, 1990*

I've always loved Steve Winwood. I used to go and see the Spencer Davis Group when I was 18 and he was about 16. He used to play really great guitar as well as great piano – I wanted to hit the little fucker, he was so good!
Dave Gilmour, *Pink Floyd, 1990*

It will be massive! It will jump out of the box and go mad. It will explode! Believe me – I know.
Terence Trent D'Arby, *1989, on* Neither Fish Nor Fowl, *his flop LP*

I'm the only genuine sex symbol in the current pop scene.
Ian McCulloch, *Echo & the Bunnymen*

We've always known we'd be huge stars, and it's all we wanted, so it won't surprise us when it happens. We don't want to be known as some fucking spaced-out Mancunians who've got nothing better to do than take drugs and make music.
Ian Brown, *Stone Roses, 1989*

We knocked off Duran Duran from Number One, then Frankie Goes to Hollywood knocked us off, then *Careless Whisper* knocked them off. I really loved all that. To tell you the truth, I never felt threatened. I must admit I never thought The Frankies would be around for very long. All the English bands were dependent on other people for songwriting, production, you name it. Nobody else was self-contained and I always realised that.
George Michael

People copy me. Look at Morrissey – he's just a carbon copy, without the humour.
Ian McCulloch, *Echo & the Bunnymen*

Bitching

Richard Branson doesn't even invite me round his house no more. That's because I usually beg for money and I hate cricket.
John Lydon, *Public Image Ltd, 1992*

I wanted to go on the road after making the last Stones album *Dirty Work*, but Her Majesty suddenly decided not to go.
Keith Richards, *1988*

The Beatles were very blasé – successful, rich. They just didn't seem to care about anything. Sure, they were very creative but somehow they just seemed to regard it all as a joke – and it was. The Beatles were so ridiculously popular, it was so stupid. They never used to play – they just used to go on making so much bread, it was crazy.
Mick Jagger, *1974*

The Beatles were so blasé and, at times, difficult. They would put up barriers which came from having too many people approaching them. They got very big-headed. It happened very quickly for them in England, they were just young guys from the provinces and didn't want to let anybody know.
Mick Jagger, *1974*

I can't stand being late. If I'm ten minutes late, I start getting upset. But none of that *discipline*. Not like some of these bands – like Deep Purple. You go in their dressing-room before a show and there's a dead silence. They're all sitting around having a glass of milk and reading the *Evening News*.
Rod Stewart

Mick's an old friend of mine. Our battles aren't exactly what people think they are. They're on many different levels – it's not just 'who runs The Rolling Stones?'
Keith Richards, *1988*

He is the most belligerent awful person ever . . . I find him a very coarse man, bordering on repulsive. He's obnoxious when he's drunk, he really is.
Deep Purple's guitarist **Ritchie Blackmore** *on Ian Gillan, 1991*

I'll tell you how drunk Blackmore is on stage every night. He marks his whisky bottles so he knows what his tolerance is, but one night I caught him falling over eating bread backstage because someone had told him dry bread sobers you up.
Ian Gillan *on Ritchie Blackmore, 1991*

I've been made almost unconscious from the fumes on stage.
Ian Gillan *on Ritchie Blackmore, 1991*

U2 are simple though, aren't they? I mean, I've said it before and I'll say it again, they're definitely simple. My window cleaner's got more to say than that cunt, let's face it.
Mark E. Smith, *1990*

A band like Spandau Ballet is totally direct and pointed. That's so boring because you see it all in one go – clothes, fashion, hair and that's it. There's nothing to discover, no mystique, no charm, no personality.
Bono, *1981*

If this was a slightly more primitive time I would already be burning at the stake. I expect there is still time for that.
Morrissey, *1989*

Wendy James looks great but she can't sing. She'd have been great in silent movies.
Mags *from Fuzzbox, 1989*

Elvis Costello is terrible, all fat and sweaty. Can't dance either.
Ian McCulloch

Every time I come back to Britain from elsewhere I get pissed off. It's the civil liberties thing. Even when people are partying on the Berlin Wall, you can't do it near the M25.
Will, *The Shamen, 1990*

I resent people you grow up admiring who turn out to be the biggest tossers, like David Bowie. I just wish he'd been killed in a car accident after he'd finished *Low*.
Robert Smith, *The Cure*

The Stone Roses album, I really like it, but it's all singing about she this and she that . . . *Never* write songs about girls.
Ian McCulloch, *1989*

Duran Duran! They're just crap. Shit. Publicly they're arseholes. They do immeasurable damage. They damage music by doing what the American cavalry did to the Indians – massacre it, kill it.
Mike Scott

Bono would love to be six foot tall and thin and good-looking. But he's not. He reminds me of a soddin' mountain goat.
Ian McCulloch

Paul Weller just stole everything. He's a skinny twat who has the worst haircut going.
Ian McCulloch

I did that first album with Keith Levine and he had a unique rhythm guitar style which has since been copied by God knows how many bands. The indie scene positively thrives on that. Even that Edge in U2 has copied it all from Keith . . . but he doesn't quite get it right, does he?
John Lydon, *Public Image Ltd, 1992*

I did Dylan, and he fucked me over. I hate that guy. That was the most miserable session, too. I did a really good job on it, and he kept my playing on there even when the advance copies went out to the record company. Then at the last moment he took it off because he said it sounded too much like Guns 'n' Roses. Why did he *call* me, y'know?
Slash, *1991*

Songs

Leonard Chess had explained that it would be better for me if I had original songs. I was very glad to hear this because I had created many extra verses for other people's songs and I was eager to do an entire creation of my own.
Chuck Berry, The Autobiography, *1987*

The story of *Heartbreak Hotel* is this: Mae Boren Axton, songwriter and Hank Snow's PR lady, was shown a newspaper clipping by her friend Tommy Durden, another songwriter. The clipping reported a suicide by a young man who left a one-line note, 'I walk a lonely street.' Axton and Durden wrote the song around the line and made a tape of it within half an hour.
Nick Tosches, Country, *1985*

I told Carl Perkins about this friend of mine in the Air Force, a black man from Virginia called C.V. White. He used to get dressed up to go to town on Saturday night with his three-day pass. He had his blue Air Force uniform with standard-issue black shoes and he'd always say, man, don't step on my blue suedes, I'm going out tonight. I'd say, C.V., hold on now, they're black Air Force issue and he'd say, Tonight, they're blue suede shoes, don't step on them. I never forgot that and I told Carl, write a song about Don't step on my blue suede shoes. He wrote it that night.
Johnny Cash, *1991*

Blue Suede Shoes was even more to the point. This had been a hit for Carl Perkins in 1956 but Elvis took it over the following year and gave it wholly new dimensions. It was important – the idea that clothes could dominate your life.
Nik Cohn, *1968*

If you find a turd in your toilet bowl, it'll be me and I'll be looking for you.
Jerry Lee Lewis's *original opening line for* It'll Be Me

I didn't have any idea that Alan Freed was being compensated for giving special attention to *Maybellene* on his radio programme by a gift from Leonard registering him part of the writer's credit to the song. In fact I didn't know then that a person also got compensation for writing as well as recording a song. My first royalty statement made me aware that some person named Russ Frato and the Alan Freed I had phoned were also part composers of the song.
Chuck Berry *learns about payola, 1955*

I was washing dishes at the Greyhound bus station at the time. I couldn't talk back to my boss man. He would bring all these pots back for me to wash, and one day I said, 'I've got to do something to stop this man bringing back all these pots to me to wash,' and I said, 'Awap bob a lup bop a wop bam boom, take 'em out!' and that's what I meant at the time. I wrote *Good Golly Miss Molly* in the kitchen, I wrote *Long Tall Sally* in that kitchen.
Little Richard

I'd been singing *Tutti Frutti* for years, but it never struck me as a song you'd *record*. I didn't go to New Orleans to record no *Tutti Frutti*. Sure, it used to crack the crowds up when I sang it in the clubs, with those risqué lyrics: Tutti Frutti, good booty/If it don't fit, don't force it/You can grease it, make it easy . . . I never thought it would be a hit, even with the lyrics cleaned up.
Little Richard

Louis Jordan's *Saturday Night Fish Fry* is the perfect record. Somewhere between jump, jazz and R & B, it is a whole way of life in one song – it shows that rock'n'roll did not start with Bill Haley.
Jerry Dammers, *The Specials*

I don't think the lyrics are that important. I remember when I was very young, this is very serious, I read an article by Fats Domino which has really influenced me. He said you should never sing the lyrics out very clearly.
Mick Jagger, *1968*

You know the song *Stray Cat Blues*? Mick told me he wrote it about a certain chick. He said he usually doesn't write like that but he had this particular one in mind. When he was in California the girl called him and said, 'Thanks for writing that song about me.' He was shocked

because he felt there was no way she could have recognised herself. But she did and it freaked him.
Devon, *supergroupie*, *1970*

Getting turned onto *Under My Thumb*, a revenge song filled with hatred for women, made me feel crazy. And it wasn't an isolated musical moment that I could frown on and forget. Because when you get to listening to male rock lyrics, the message to women is devastating. We are cunts.
Susan Hiwatt, *Twenty Minute Fandangos*

This voice was like broken glass, like spitting. The words were like arrows, being shot straight into the heart of the establishment. That was what made me realise what the words of a song could do.
Bernie Taupin on *hearing Bob Dylan sing* The Times They Are A-Changin' *on Radio Luxembourg in 1964*

I think songs should be disposable. I can't even remember some of the words or chords of albums we did two years ago, like *Tumbleweed Connection*. To me songs are like postage stamps. You lick them, put them on a letter, and never see them again.
Elton John, *1973*

The words just came into my head: 'She packed my bags last night, pre-flight. Zero-hour is nine a.m.' I remember jumping out of the car and running into my parents' house, shouting, 'Please don't anyone talk to me until I've written this down.'
Bernie Taupin on Rocket Man

I had no melody, so I only sang the lines I'd written for four or five bars at a time. Having sung one line, I'd take a breath and do the same thing again, and so on to the end. I never knew the complete melody until I'd finished the song and played the whole thing back.
David Bowie on Heroes

This song put me in the middle of the road. Travelling there soon became a bore so I headed for the ditch. A rougher ride, but I saw more interesting people there.
Neil Young's Decade *(1977) liner note on his 1972 hit* Heart of Gold

I've written most of my best songs driving on a long journey scribbling lyrics on cigarette packets whilst steering.
Neil Young, *1990*

My brother Dennis came home from school one day and he said,
'Listen, you guys, it looks like surfing's going to be the next big craze
and you guys ought to write a song about it.'
Brian Wilson *of The Beach Boys*

I was on my way to DJ at the Bel Air when I wrote *Careless Whisper*. I
have always written on buses, trains and in cars. These days it's planes
– but for me writing has always been about boredom and movement. It
always happens on journeys.
George Michael

I never regretted stepping back from the songwriting. Number one, he
didn't need the help. Number two, he didn't want it.
Andrew Ridgeley

I would say 50 per cent to 70 per cent of all songs we cut come out of a
conversation. They don't come out of David Porter going home and
sweating, staying up until three in the morning, sitting up trying to
think of a title. It comes natural, the natural things are the ones we
hang on to.
Steve Cropper, *guitarist with Booker T & the MGs*

I can remember a conversation that Otis and I had about life: we were
speaking about life in general, the ups and downs, and what have you.
I said, 'What you are griping about, you're on the road all the time, all
you can look for is a little respect when you come home.' He wrote the
tune from our conversation. We laughed about it quite a few times. In
fact, Otis laughed about it all the way to the bank.
Al Jackson Jr, *drummer with Booker T & the MGs*

I find it very easy to write lyrics. I've always written 10 per cent too
many words for a song, because I think people only listen to every third
or fourth word.
Ray Davies, *1989*

Lot of the songs I wrote from hearin' people talk. I go along some times
and I hear people say words and I pick up from that. You got to listen
to the words in the street, man, that's where you get the songs from.
Muddy Waters, *1974*

Long Distance Call, that came from when I was on a street-car in Chicago and I asked a little girl for her number, you know, and she gave me a number. I called the number, it was the county morgue.
Muddy Waters, *1974*

Those first five or six songs that I wrote, I was just taking notes at a fantastic rock concert that was going on inside my head. And once I had written the songs, I had to sing them.
Jim Morrison

I rang Edge the other night and told him I'd discovered this thing called The Song. U2 never wrote songs as such. We used to structure pieces of music, working in terms of atmosphere, texture and tones.
Bono, *1985*

I saw an episode of *Star Trek* about a year ago which used a line from a Bob Dylan song, and I do the same thing myself. I can get it from anywhere. A remark, a headline, you put some words together that stick in your head. The art is in telling what's good and what's bad. What'll work, and what won't.
Bap Kennedy, *Energy Orchard, 1992*

Don't You Want Me was a story in a women's magazine. The first two lines were the first two lines in this story. It was called *Intimate Romance* or something, an American import. It wasn't actually a waitress in the story, it was 'I was working in a bus station' or something, and somehow they summed up a person's whole life in a sentence. It was really good, so I pinched it.
Phil Oakey, *Human League, 1990*

Waits is an originator without being the least bit original. He was the first in a long line of white spade urban rock'n'roll poets who chose to romanticise the sleazy side of the tracks. This approach had been done to death in the literature of the Beat Generation, but Waits was the first to successfully bring it above ground on vinyl.
Terri A. Huggins

Every generation needs its derelict. Mom and Dad had Dean Martin; we've got Tom Waits.
Terri A. Huggins

I'm not a moody songwriter. I don't need to go the Caribbean to produce. It's a gift from God, it just comes.
Smokey Robinson, *1992*

Writing songs . . . a greater source of anxiety I have yet to encounter.
Chrissie Hynde, *1990*

I think you're in trouble if your videos are better than your songs.
Boy George

We booked two or three weeks to do the songwriting (for *Waking Up With The House On Fire*) and didn't use one day of it. We had an argument and we left. We rowed and rowed and George smashed his tape recorder and I threw a chair at him. Then we wrote the album in four days.
Jon Moss

While too big to be bossed about, George had also been too busy being a star to find anything but the circumstances of his fame to write songs about. It's a classic trap and he fell into it head first.
Dave Rimmer

I always make sure I have a guitar around. I might suddenly get an idea for a song. I don't sit around saying: Now I'm going to write a song. They come to me. I firmly believe they're all floating through the room right now. You don't create them, you find them and nurture them.
Keith Richards, *1991*

I think he's an excellent lyric writer. I've never been able to come to terms with his melodies. I'm a sucker for an old-fashioned melody and I find his very disparate. They tail off a lot.
David Bowie, *1989, on Morrissey*

I like that first John Lennon album a hell of a lot. I think all the songs are really beautifully written and very straight from the shoulder. There's an honesty in the lyrics there.
David Bowie, *1989*

I think Lou writes in a much more detached manner from me. Lou's the kind of guy who sits back and watches what's going on and takes notes . . . He's a natural journalist. He's almost become a kind of musical Woody Allen.
David Bowie, *1989*

51

What's made Jackson Browne more acceptable than most other singer-songwriters is the likelihood that he's the Joni Mitchell for teenage boys. His best songs aim for the heart of the suburban adolescent experience: romance in the shopping centres, vulnerability behind the bowling alley. Those with the sensitivity can gauge their emotional turnarounds through his songs the way many (men and women) identify with Joni.
Wayne Robins, Creem, *1975*

Everything You Did is dead serious about those kinky little domestic psychodramas Randy Newman is so funny about. The rest are those little substitutes for crossword puzzles that are harder to figure out because there isn't any answer. Dylan has a lot to answer for. He made bad poets think songs could be about anything (or nothing) that ran through their uniquely beautiful minds.
Joe Goldberg, Creem, *1976, on Steely Dan*, The Royal Scam

If I knew where to go for good songs. I'd go there more often. Certainly being slow is no sign of excellence; I'm not promoting my stuff on the basis of the labour, but my words don't come out any faster than metal from a mine. On the last album there's a translation from a poem by Lorca. Just rendering his words in English took nearly 200 hours.
Leonard Cohen, 1991

Words aren't the salad dressing on the meal of music. Words are the first thing for me. I like having a finished lyric that I'm pleased with, and letting the music follow from there.
Mike Scott, The Waterboys

Originally, the function of songs was devotional, I think. Then in the balladeering centuries, they became a vehicle for the spreading of information, stories and opinions. Now in the 20th century they have become a way of making money and achieving fame. I think the other two purposes are much better.
Mike Scott

C. S. Lewis once said that no one wrote the books he wanted to read, so he wrote them himself. That's all I'm doing, that's all I've ever done.
Mike Scott

Ostensibly, the subject of the song is truckdriving, but anybody who thinks that *Willin'* is just a song about truckdriving probably also thinks that Raymond Chandler's Philip Marlowe books are *about* a detective.
Charles Shaar Murray, *1975, on the song by Lowell George*

I hate to come to a town and be out the next day. You never get to find out about the street, and what's going down, and if there's a song out there to be written.
Lowell George, *1975*

Back before the flood, when Patti Smith began caterwauling poetry above an electric guitar, she probably didn't realise she was clearing the path for legions of bad-tempered demoiselles with dark clothing and three-subject notebooks full of lousy poems.
Steve Anderson, Village Voice, *1982*

I write at the microphone. With pen and paper I start on the things I suppose I should be writing about rather than what I feel.
Bono, *1982*

I often use words not for what they mean but for what they sound like, the way they bump up against other words or things like that. I'm more interested in impression than detail at the moment. I'd like to start using everyday speech.
Bono, *1984*

This album covers the break-up of my marriage, the relationship afterwards with Rosanna Arquette, which also broke up, and a period of therapy during which for five years I had to look at a lot of stuff that I found very difficult. It was a struggle. And part of that I had to put in the songs.
Peter Gabriel *on* Us, *1992*

A record doesn't detail a person's changes. If I make a record, that's it. It doesn't affect how I live. And it *isn't* how I live. It doesn't affect my life, and my life doesn't affect it. What can you say on 40 minutes of wax?
Van Morrison, *1973*

Whatever changes happen to you are reflected and expressed in the songs you write. Beyond that, it's nobody else's business. I think that's a decent, honourable line to draw and if anybody crosses that line, I'll kick their head in. I'm a pacifist until you come into my house, and then I'll kill your children.
Elvis Costello, *1989*

I loved Shane McGowan's attack on it all and his ability to write lyrics about today in a very traditional way.
Terry Woods, *The Pogues, 1989*

What's special about U2 is the music, not the musician. I and the others are just ordinary people and our trade is to make music. Somebody else's is to build houses or work in a factory or teach. We're just getting to grips with our trade as songwriters.
Bono, *1987*

The second album is more aggressive and it's not got the warmth that the first one had. It really sounds like a touring album. Its subject matter is a lot of shagging and general debauchery.
Mick Hucknall, *1989*

I find my stuff is filled with compassion. It's one of the things that I see thematically running through these lyrics. There's a lot of things that I'm describing that seem personal and painful but, as a literate person, I know they're universals. You can't beat Shakespeare – *Hamlet*, for Chrissakes! No one treats *Hamlet* like a personal aberration of Shakespeare.
Lou Reed, *1992*

I spend the bulk of my time taking things out. I'm alway trying to get a visual image you can get really quickly. When you hear the record, it shoots by, so I want you to get the image quick. And if you didn't, then it's bad writing.
Lou Reed, *1992*

Springsteen's songs capture and celebrate a working class in transition; people hit by unemployment and disillusion, people at the bottom in an uncaring country that promises freedom but doesn't deliver it. He generates a sense of community which is his great gift to the world.
Jon Savage

I think that the irony on our songs has always been overrated. It's the thing we're really, really famous for.
Neil Tennant, *Pet Shop Boys, 1992*

I love Tom Waits. I think he's the great talent of the last ten years as far as dealing with America in a real way.
The Edge, *U2, 1988*

It started out as just a little thing, *Sad-Eyed Lady Of The Lowland*, but I got carried away, somewhere along the line. I just sat down at a table and started writing. At the session itself. And I just started writing and I couldn't stop. After a period of time, I forgot what it was all about, and I started trying to get back to the beginning.
Bob Dylan, *1969*

The Fifties

Rock'n'roll is the most brutal, ugly, vicious form of expression – sly, lewd, in plain fact, dirty . . . rancid-smelling, aphrodisiac . . . the martial music of every delinquent on the face of the earth.
Frank Sinatra, *1957*

Our airways have been flooded in recent years with whining guitarists, musical riots put to switchblade beat, obscure lyrics about hugging, squeezing, and rocking all night long.
Vance Packard, *author of* The Hidden Persuaders, *at a press conference in Washington, 1957*

Most of the best early rockers came out of the South – Elvis from Mississippi, Little Richard from Georgia, Buddy Holly from Texas, Jerry Lee Lewis from Louisiana, Gene Vincent from Virginia. These were the states where the living had always been meanest, where teenagers had been least catered for, and, where, therefore, the pop kickback was now most frantic.
Nik Cohn, *1968*

Ubangi Stomp typified the tough, churlish strain of country music that evolved in the 1950s. Known as rockabilly, it was the music of men such as Elvis Presley, Carl Perkins and Jerry Lee Lewis. Aflash with images of sex, violence, and redneck existentialism, rockabilly was the glorious fluorescence of white rock and roll. It seemed such a sexy, pagan horror, such a dangerous new creature, that America feared it, preached against it, and tried to ban it.
Nick Tosches, Country, *1985*

His great gift was that, no matter how frantic he got, his voice remained controlled and drawling country. He seemed to have a lot of time to spare, an unshakeable ease, and this gave him class.
Nik Cohn *on Jerry Lee Lewis, 1968*

What made rockabilly such a drastically new music was its spirit, a thing that bordered on mania. Elvis's *Good Rockin' Tonight* was not merely a party song, but an invitation to a holocaust. Junior Parker's

Mystery Train was an eerie shuffle; Elvis's *Mystery Train* was a demonic incantation.
Nick Tosches

Age doesn't matter back home. You can marry at ten if you find a husband.
Myra Lewis, *first of Jerry Lee's wives*

'I was born feet first, been rockin' ever since,' he'll tell you if he's in a good mood. His vassals and kin will tell you more: Jerry Lee can out-drink, out-dope, out-fight, out-cuss, out-shoot and out-fuck any man alive. He is the last American wild man, *homo agrestis americanus ultimus*.
Nick Tosches, Country, *1985*

Out of all the great Southern rockers, just about the most splendid was the before-mentioned Little Richard Penniman out of Macon, Georgia, who was and still is the most exciting live performer I ever saw in my life.
Nik Cohn, *1968*

My music made your liver quiver, your bladder spatter, your knees freeze. And your big toe shoot right up in your boot.
Little Richard

He'd scream and scream and scream. He had a freak voice, tireless, hysterical, completely indestructible, and he never in his life sang at anything lower than an enraged bull-like roar. On every phrase, he'd embroider with squeals, rasps, siren whoops. His stamina, his drive were limitless.
Nik Cohn, *1968, on Little Richard*

I'm just the same as ever – loud, electrifying and full of personal magnetism.
Little Richard

As a person he was brash, fast, bombastic, a sort of prototype Muhammed Ali.
Nik Cohn, *1968, on Little Richard*

True rock and roll is really my thing, it's nothing but an outpouring of my soul, it's me. I created that. When they come to me, they see history, they see a living legend on the stage.
Little Richard

I've worked with some top artists, Presley, all those, and nobody's ever had that kind of magic.
H. B. Barnum, *sax player*, The Life and Times of Little Richard, *by Charles White, 1984*

You knew not, night to night, where he was going to come from. He'd just burst onto the stage from anywhere and you wouldn't be able to hear anything but the roar of the audience. He might come out and walk on the piano. He might go out in the audience. His charisma was just a whole new thing to the business. Richard was totally out of this world, wild, and it gave people who wanted to scream a chance to go ahead and scream instead of trying to be cool.
H.B. Barnum, *sax player*

Mick Jagger used to sit at the side of the stage watching my act. Every performance. They had a little record out, a cover of Chuck Berry's *Come On*, but they had never done a tour before. Mick opened the show with The Rolling Stones. They were making $50 a night. He couldn't even pay for his room. Mick used to talk to me all the time. He'd sit there and talk all night if I let him. He and the others used to sleep on Bo Diddley's floor in the hotel.
Little Richard

He drove the whole house into a complete frenzy. There's no single phrase to describe his hold on the audience. It might excite some and terrify others. It's hypnotic, like an evangelistic meeting where, for want of a better phrase, Richard is the disciple and the audience the flock that follows. I couldn't believe the power of Little Richard on stage. He was amazing.
Mick Jagger

The very first time I saw Little Richard work I couldn't believe my own eyes or ears!
Gene Vincent

Chuck Berry was possibly the finest of all rockers and he's easily my favourite pop writer ever. He wrote endless Teen Romance lyrics but sang them with vicious, sly cynicism and this is the clash that makes him so funny, so attractive.
Nik Cohn, *1968*

Buddy Holly was called Charles Hardin Holly and first came out of Lubbock, Texas, with broken teeth, wire glasses, halitosis, plus every

last possible kind of country Southernness. He wasn't appetizing. In fact, he was an obvious no-hoper . . . So a man called Lloyd Greenfield, a toughened Northern agent, took him up and changed him into another person. Buddy had his teeth capped, his breath cleansed, his hair styled, his wire glasses exchanged for big impressive black ones, his voice toned. Then he was put into high-school sweaters and taught how to smile. Suddenly, he was all-America.
Nik Cohn, *1968*

Buddy Holly was the gentleman of rockabilly, the first soft rocker.
Nick Tosches

I always loved Roy. I looked up to the way he was, admired the way he handled himself. That aloofness he had influenced me profoundly. It was the way he carried himself, y'know, with this benign dignity. His music was always more important than the media. It wasn't a fashion statement. It wasn't about being in the right place at the right time making the right moves. That didn't matter to Roy. Just like it doesn't matter to me.
Neil Young, *1990, on Roy Orbison*

When Richard first arrived in Hollywood, he was so far out! His hair was processed a foot high on his head. His shirt was so loud it looked as though he had drunk raspberry juice, cherryade, malt, and greens and then thrown up all over himself. Man, he was a freak.
Bumps Blackwell, *his producer-songwriter-manager*

I saw Howlin' Wolf and Elmore James for the first time on 47th Street, a tour I'll never lose memory of. I didn't want to leave the place where Elmore James was performing but Ralph had seen these artists before and insisted that we try other places. At the Palladium on Wabush Avenue we looked up and found the Marquee glowing with MUDDY WATERS TONIGHT. Ralph gave me the lead as we ran up the stairs to the club, knowing I sang Muddy's songs and that he was my favourite blues singer. We paid our 50-cents admission and scrimmaged forward to the bandstand, where in true living colour I saw Muddy Waters.
Chuck Berry, The Autobiography, *1987*

Richard opened the door. He brought the races together. When I first went on the road there were many segregated audiences. With Richard, although they still had the audiences segregated in the building, they were *there* together. And most times, before the end of the night, they would all be mixed together.
H.B. Barnum, *sax player*

I will never forget Jimi loading his belongings on the bus. His guitar was wrapped in a potato sack. It had only five strings on it.
Henry Nash, *backing vocalist, recalls Hendrix joining Little Richard's band*

Richard taught Hendrix a lot of things, and Hendrix copied a lot of things from Richard. That's where he got the charisma. Richard used to say, 'Look, don't be ashamed to do whatever you feel.'
Marquette, *road manager*

Like once with Little Richard, me and another guy got fancy shirts 'cause we were tired of wearing the uniform. Richard called a meeting. 'I am Little Richard, the King,' he said. 'King of Rock and Rhythm. I am the only one allowed to be pretty. Take off those shirts.' Man, it was all like that. Bad pay, lousy living, and getting burned.
Jimi Hendrix

Jerry Lee learned how to rock'n'roll from me. He was just a country singer till he heard my songs and he recorded a lot of them.
Little Richard

James Brown was different from me. He was big to the black market. When he came to town you would get 10,000 blacks. When I came to town you would get 10,000 whites, and about ten blacks.
Little Richard

Richard would never slow down his work rate. Denver now. Denver is at a high elevation. But rather than tame the show down, he would ingest large amounts of bottled oxygen between sets to keep his heart going.
Bill House, *lead guitarist*

I've paid almost two million dollars worth of dues, but I still didn't cheat nobody. I was cheated, but didn't cheat nobody.
Little Richard

I put James Brown in show business and he never mentioned my name. I put Joe Tex in the business, I put Jimi Hendrix in the business – he played in my band for two years before he made a record, I put Don Covay in the business, Otis Redding was in the business because of me, Billy Preston met The Beatles through me – it was in *Time* magazine last week.
Little Richard, 1969

Elvis

If I could find a white man who had the Negro sound and Negro feel, I could make a billion dollars.
Sam Phillips, *Sun Records*

The reason I taped Elvis was this: Over and over I remember Sam saying, 'If only I could find a white man who had the Negro feel, I could make a billion dollars.' This is what I heard in Elvis, this . . . what I guess they now call 'soul', this Negro sound.
Marion Keisker *of the Memphis Recording Service, explains why she made a tape copy of a $4 demo, which the 19-year-old truckdriver had recorded directly onto an acetate disc*

What rock needed to get it off the ground now was a universal hero, a symbol, a rallying point . . . Obviously, Bill Haley didn't measure up. Equally obviously, Elvis Presley did.
Nik Cohn, Awbopbopaloobop, *1968*

It is vital to remember that Elvis was the first young Southern white to sing rock'n'roll, something he copied from no one but made up on the spot; and to know that even though other singers would have come up with a white version of the new black music acceptable to teenage America, of all that did emerge in Elvis's wake, none sang as powerfully, or with more than a touch of his magic.
Greil Marcus

The teddy boys were waiting for Elvis Presley. Everybody under 20 all over the world was waiting.
Jeff Nuttall, Bomb Culture, *1968*

I just want to tell y'all not to worry – them people in New York and Hollywood are not gonna change me none.
Elvis *to crowd at charity concert, Memphis, July 1956*

If the police had not been there, forming a blue wall around the stage, the audience might have eaten Elvis's body in a Eucharistic frenzy. They were his and he was theirs, their leader: it was an incandescent moment.
Stanley Booth, Esquire, *1968, on the charity concert*

Elvis had tried to go on being himself. When Paramount offered him a movie contract with a clause forbidding him to ride motorcycles, he said, 'I'd rather not make movies.' They let him keep his motorcycles.
Stanley Booth, Esquire, *1968*

I knew Elvis was going to be a monster the first time I saw him perform because everybody had to watch him, the men as well as the women. Even all us other performers would crowd backstage to watch him. Elvis was a great rhythm guitar player and that influenced me but I never tried to twist or shake like him.
Johnny Cash, *1991*

Elvis Presley recorded a song of mine. That's the one recording I treasure the most . . . it was called *Tomorrow Is A Long Time*.
Bob Dylan, *1969*

Elvis Presley is a supreme figure in American life, one whose presence, no matter how banal or predictable, brooks no real comparisons.
Greil Marcus, Mystery Train, *1977*

Elvis has fulfilled the American dream: he is young, rich, famous, adored. Hardly a day passes in Memphis without a politician wanting to name something after him. So far nothing has been found worthy of the honour. Presley has become a young man of whom his city and his country can truly be proud.
Stanley Booth, Esquire, *1968*

This was the major teen breakthrough and Elvis triggered it. In this way, without even trying, he became one of the people who have radically affected the way that people think and live.
Nik Cohn

Elvis has emerged as great *artist*, a great *rocker*, a great *purveyor of schlock*, a great *heart throb*, a great *bore*, a great *symbol of potency*, a great *ham*, a great *nice person*, and, yes, a great American.
Greil Marcus, Mystery Train, *1977*

Elvis is where pop begins and ends. He's the great original and, even now, he's the image that makes all others seem shoddy, the boss. For once, the fan club spiel is justified: Elvis is King.
Nik Cohn

Before Elvis, rock had been a gesture of vague rebellion. Once he'd happened, it immediately became solid, self-contained, and then it spawned its own style in clothes and language and sex, a total independence in almost everything – all the things that are now taken for granted.
Nik Cohn

A self-made man is rather boring, but a self-made king is something else. Dressed in blue, red, white, ultimately gold, with a superman cape and covered with jewels no one can be sure are fake, Elvis might epitomise the worst of our culture – he is bragging, selfish, narcissistic, condescending, materialistic to the point of insanity.
Greil Marcus

He would come out on stage standing on a golden Cadillac. He wore a golden suit, and on his feet, he had golden slippers. His sideboards reached down to his earlobes and his hair, heavy with grease, came up in a great ducktail plume off his forehead. He had a lopsided grin and he used it all the time.
Nik Cohn

What links the greatest rock'n'roll careers is a volcanic ambition, a lust for more than anyone has a right to expect.
Greil Marcus

At the gate Jerry Lee Lewis leaned against his 1976 Lincoln Continental. He held a .38 calibre Derringer, and he was drunk. He had come to liberate Elvis, to speak with Elvis, to sing with Elvis. He demanded Elvis come to the gate. Then he demanded he be brought in to Elvis. He waved the gun and yelled curses.
Nick Tosches on *Jerry Lee's arrest outside Graceland in 1976*

If Elvis had the imagination to come up with the dreams that kept him going, he had the music to bring them to life, and make them real to huge numbers of other people. It was the genius of his singing, an ease and intensity that has no parallel in American music, that along with his dreams separated him from his context.
Greil Marcus

Imagine, then, what Elvis Presley, 19-year-old truckdriver of Memphis, Tennessee, would have thought if somehow he could've had some prescient flash of Elvis Presley, 42-year-old superstar of Memphis, Tennessee, killing his pain with an obscene blend of cheeseburgers and scag. If they could meet, the one with everything to come, the other with everything gone . . . would they still know each other?
Charles Shaar Murray, 1977

The kind of stardom that was visited on Elvis Presley was simply more than he could handle.
Charles Shaar Murray, 1977

We went to see him do a show, but it was absolutely pitiful. He was so drugged, he could hardly sing – he just stood there, handing out scarves. Then we were taken backstage to meet him. There was this dressing-room, full of Memphis Mafia, with Elvis in the middle of them on a stool, wrapped in towels. He looked awful, he was sweating, with the dye from his hair running down his face. And all these guys in suits around him in a huddle. I don't think he even knew who we were. As we walked away afterwards Elton said, 'He's not long for this world.'
Bernie Taupin, 1976

The awful spectacle of a great star, falling apart among servants and minders, shocked Elton to the core.
Philip Norman

Elvis never revealed himself. He was found dead on his bathroom floor early on the morning of August 16, 1977, at the age of 42. Traces of 13 different drugs were found in his system – grim corroboration of the sensational allegations that had been published less than a month before in a hastily-written paperback called *Elvis: What Happened?* by three former Presley lackeys.
Nick Tosches

Elvis is the dream gone wrong, that's why as a character he's so fascinating. His demise was such a public one. He was for a lot of people the definition of America, all its promise, all it could achieve and all the freedom of the country.
The Edge, U2, 1988

Mini-tycoon Jonathan King, radiantly happy to be in front of the cameras even on such a solemn occasion, said that this was a doubly important death because the man doing the dying had been entirely created by the media. Tony Palmer said it would be a pity to leave the audience with the impression that anyone as talented as Elvis Presley had been entirely created by the media. Jonathan King said, 'I agree with Tony Palmer.'
Clive James *on the Thames TV tribute*, The Observer, *1977*

The book is a prodigy of bad writing, excitable, sarcastic and only fleetingly literate. It is also as exploitative as the exploiters whom Goldman reviles, and no more tasteful than an Elvis jumpsuit.
Martin Amis *on* Elvis, *by Albert Goldman*

At his best Elvis not only embodies but personalizes so much of what is good about this place: a delight in sex that is sometimes simple, sometimes complex, but always open; a love of roots and a respect for the past; a rejection of the past and a demand for novelty; the kind of racial harmony that for Elvis, a white man, means a profound affinity with the nuances of black culture combined with an equally profound understanding of his own whiteness; a burning desire to get rich, and to have fun; a natural affection for big cars, flashy clothes, for the symbols of status that give pleasure both as symbols, and on their own terms.
Greil Marcus, Mystery Train, *1977*

The wonder of Elvis will never die; no carrion bird can kill it. There was more mystery, more power, in Elvis, singer of *Danny Boy*, than in Bob Dylan, utterer of hermetic ironies. It is the sheer superhuman tastelessness of Elvis that shakes the mind.
Nick Tosches

One thing is certain. In an age bereft of magic, Elvis was one of the last great mysteries, the secret of which lay unrevealed even to himself. That he failed, fatally, to understand that mystery, gives anyone else little hope of doing so. After all, the truest mysteries are those without explanations.
Nick Tosches

His mother had been the one, perhaps the only one, who had told him throughout his life that even though he came from poor country people, he was just as good as anyone. His success had not surprised her, nor had it changed her. Shortly after Gladys Presley was buried, her husband and son were standing on the magnificent front steps at

Graceland. 'Look, Daddy,' Elvis sobbed, pointing to the chickens his mother had kept on a lawn of the $100,000 mansion, 'Mama won't never feed them chickens no more.'
Stanley Booth, Esquire, *1968*

The Beatles

The very first tune I ever learned to play was *That'll Be The Day*. My mother taught me to play it on the banjo, sitting there with endless patience until I managed to work out all the chords.
John Lennon

I can remember what it was like waiting for Gene Vincent, and thinking: He's coming! He's coming!
John Lennon

I think John had a great wanderlust. He had an extremely adventurous streak. You could see that the way he behaved. He always tackled everything head on with the greatest of confidence.
Paul McCartney

This boy at school had been to Holland. He said he'd got this record at home by somebody called Little Richard who was better than Elvis. Elvis was bigger than religion in my life. We used go to this boy's house after school and listen to 78s. We'd buy five Senior Service loose in this shop and some chips and go along. The new record was *Long Tall Sally*. When I heard it, it was so great I couldn't speak. You know how you are torn. I didn't want to leave Elvis. We all looked at each other but I didn't want to say anything against Elvis, even in my mind.
John Lennon

My family was from the housing estate, like the rest of The Beatles. My dad was a cotton salesman and my mum was a midwife and we lived in a council house that went with her job. John's relations were definitely middle-class.
Paul McCartney

I lost my mother twice. Once as a child of five and then again at 17. It made me very, very bitter inside. I had just begun to re-establish a relationship with her when she was killed. We'd caught up on so much in just a few short years.
John Lennon on his mother's death in a car accident, 1958

At the time, the group was just another of the more than 300 rock 'n' roll beatnik bands working around Liverpool – a situation emphasised by the number of names with which they experimented. Among these were The Cavemen, The Moondogs, The Moonshiners, and during the period in which anglicized Kentucky Bluegrass became popular, The Quarrymen Skiffle Group.
Arnold Shaw, The Rock Revolution, *1968*

Quite a change had come over Stu, too. Astrid was now making all his clothes, including a collarless sports jacket similar to the ones Pierre Cardin had popularized in Paris. Astrid had also talked Stu into combing his hair forward over his forehead and cutting it into bowl-shaped fringe. One by one, except for Pete Best, the other boys soon followed suit, and the Beatle haircut was born.
Peter Brown on Hamburg 1960 and bass player Stu Sutcliffe's art student-photographer friend Astrid Kirchherr

There in the centre tunnel on a raised platform was a sight that galvanized him. It was in the most specific way a personification of his secret sexual desires. On stage were four young men dressed in leather trousers and jackets. They played good time rock and roll and joked with each other with macho camaraderie.
Peter Brown on Brian Epstein's first visit to the Cavern Club, 9 November 1961

What the 27-year-old Sibelius man saw was scarcely believable. The entertainers seemed oblivious to any notion of stage decorum. Between songs they smoked, ate and generally took a mischievous delight in insulting members of the audience.
Johnny Rogan on Epstein at the Cavern

Our peak for playing live was in Hamburg. At the time we weren't famous and people came to see us simply because of our music and the atmosphere we created. We got very tight as a band in those four clubs we played in Hamburg.
George Harrison

On this trip John managed to surpass his previous craziness. One night he walked onstage naked with a toilet seat around his neck to the cheers of the audience.
Peter Brown on Star Club, Hamburg, April 1961

Brian did not find the city of Hamburg with its whores and thugs as enchanting as The Beatles obviously did. He couldn't fathom out the boys' constant preoccupation with prostitutes, considering the rate they contracted venereal diseases.
Peter Brown

I remember how excited The Beatles were to meet Richard. He had been their idol for years. In Hamburg they'd always be with him asking him questions about America, the cities, the stars, the movies, Elvis, and all that. And when Richard left to go back to the United States they cried.
Billy Preston

I developed a specially close relationship with Paul McCartney, but me and John couldn't make it. John had a nasty personality. He was different from Paul and George, they were sweet.
Little Richard

Rock'n'roll is the music that inspired me to play music. There is nothing conceptually better than rock'n'roll. No group, be it The Beatles, Dylan or The Stones have ever improved on *Whole Lotta Shakin'* for my money. Or maybe, like our parents, that's my period and I'll dig it and never leave it.
John Lennon

Even the usually acerbic John Lennon was completed overawed upon learning that George Martin had worked closely with his heroes the Goons.
Johnny Rogan on the EMI audition, 6 June 1962

The boys want you out of the group. They don't think you're a good enough drummer.
Brian Epstein gives Pete Best the bad news

It's taken them two years to find out I'm not a good enough drummer?
Pete Best

His place in history was already reserved as the most luckless of all might-have-beens. In the next 24 months, The Beatles would gross £17 million. Pete Best became a baker, earning £8 a week, and married a girl named Kathy who worked at the biscuit counter at Woolworths.
Peter Brown

At the age of 22, when he was asked to join The Beatles, Ringo Starr was an unlikely candidate to sign on as a character player in the greatest bit part ever written. He was short, skinny and unassuming, with a homely countenance and sad blue eyes. Up until this point, his life had been a gothic horror story of misfortune.
Peter Brown

When we first came down to London we felt like real provincials. But it really was a great period, we were like kings of the jungle. It was probably the *best* period, actually, fame-wise. We didn't get mobbed so much. It reminded me of an exclusive men's smoking club, you know, only with The Stones, Eric Burdon, and us as members. It was just a very, very good scene.
John Lennon

Paul also persevered in educating himself. He read, he went to foreign films. He became sophisticated and, in a certain sense, very bourgeois.
Peter Brown on 1966

It was principally from the Ashers that Paul imbibed that awareness of classic and avant-garde music that led The Beatles to move away from pop rock and launch themselves on the rising tide of art rock.
Albert Goldman, 1988

The song chosen for the A side was called *Love Me Do*, the one with the banal lyrics that Paul had written when he was 16. He was greatly enhanced by a catchy harmonica riff played by John on the harmonica he had shoplifted in Arnhem.
Peter Brown

I've always said that boy could do anything he set his mind to.
John's Aunt Mimi on *hearing* Love Me Do

Gentlemen, you have just recorded your first Number One.
George Martin on Please Please Me

Will the people in the cheaper seats clap your hands, the rest of you can just rattle your jewellery.
John Lennon to audience at Royal Command Performance, Prince of Wales Theatre, 1963

BEATLEMANIA!
The Daily Mirror *describes pandemonium in streets outside London Palladium, 13 October 1963*

It was the beginning of an extraordinary period of tolerance and discretion by Fleet Street, previously accorded only to members of the Royal Family.
Peter Brown on the birth of Julian to Cynthia and John, seven months after their marriage

As The Beatles stepped out of their plane at Kennedy Airport on February 7, their first LP, *Meet The Beatles*, occupied the Number One position on bestseller charts. A squad of 120 policemen battled 5,000 rampaging teenagers.
Arnold Shaw on 1964

When the plane door opened, the screaming of the fans was louder than the sound of the jet engines.
Peter Brown, Kennedy Airport

Britannia Rules Airwaves
Variety *headline, February 1964*

The Beatles did nothing less miraculous than sweep up at least 80 per cent of the youth of the world's wealthy countries. The Beatles made rock a punk religion. They reversed the desired effects of rock music. This is unbelievably significant, because heretofore rock'n'roll had always been a calmative; it appeased youth. Sure, you were supposed to 'rip it up' on Saturday night, but you were never supposed to rip it up all of the time.
Nick Tosches, The Punk Muse

Some people began to regard their musical ability as having a god-like power. Desperate parents with ill and crippled children would come to the stage door, begging The Beatles to touch them so that they could be healed. The power of Beatlemania began to terrify them. They wanted to run away and become normal people again.
Julia Baird, Lennon's half-sister, 1988

I had an incredible conversation once with Paul McCartney. The difference between the way Lennon and McCartney behave with the people that are around them is incredible. What Lennon does is that he sits down, immediately acknowledges the fact that he's John Lennon and that everything for the rest of the night is going to revolve around him. He just completely relaxes, and lets everybody feel at ease.
Pete Townshend, 1968

My little rebellion was to have my tie loose, with the top button of my shirt undone, but Paul's always come up to me and put it straight.
John Lennon, 1969

It took a long, long time for the magnitude of it to sink in. Nicky Byrne's personal income alone, Brian estimated, could add up to five million dollars. Brian was sick. *They had given it away!* An incomprehensible sum signed away for nothing. He wondered what The Beatles would say when they found out.
Peter Brown on Epstein's merchandising blunder

The *Citizen Kane* of juke-box movies.
Andrew Sarris, American film critic, on A Hard Day's Night, *1964*

With *A Hard Day's Night* playing simultaneously in 500 American movie theatres, Beatlemania had now reached its epileptic apogee. To reduce the danger at airports, the party flew by night on a chartered Lockheed Elektra, but even at two a.m. the terminals would be swarming with kids.
Albert Goldman, The Lives of John Lennon, *1988*

I've met them. Delightful lads. Absolutely no talent.
Noel Coward

We're kidding you, we're kidding ourselves, we're kidding everybody. We don't take anything seriously except the money.
John Lennon

It was with bitter irony that The Beatles realized their audiences screamed so loudly during their concerts that the music couldn't be heard at all . . . For some of the concerts The Beatles didn't even bother to sing.
Peter Brown on the 26-date American tour, August 1964

Director Richard Lester certainly knew that The Beatles were stoned on marijuana for most of the filming. Their continuous giggling, plus their periodic trips to the dressing trailer to 'have a laugh', was enough of a clue without the tell-tale sweet scent that followed them around. The seeds that Bob Dylan had planted the previous summer had by now blossomed in the minds of four full-blown potheads.
Peter Brown on Help, *the second movie*

Compared to most performers, they handled themselves with such flippancy and frivolity that they seemed more of a triumph of manner over music.
Arnold Shaw

I got a message on acid that you should destroy your ego. And I did – I destroyed myself.
John Lennon

I must have taken a thousand trips. I just ate it all the time like candy.
John Lennon

Yoko's *grande atrocité* occurred one night when she turned up at a Transcendental Meditation lecture John and Cynthia were attending in London. When it was over she followed them out of the lecture hall and into the back seat of John's psychedelically hand-painted Rolls-Royce limousine and sat herself down between them.
Peter Brown on an incident in 1967

Christianity will go. It will vanish and shrink. I needn't argue about that. I'm right and will be proved right. We're more popular than Jesus now. I don't know which will go first – rock'n'roll or Christianity. Jesus was all right, but his disciples were thick and ordinary.
John Lennon, 1966

The rock hero must be like a lion tamer who every time he enters the cage is prepared to impose his will upon the will of the beast. It was in this will to command that The Beatles were most deficient. They were charmers in an arena where only power is respected. They had never exhibited the theatrical prowess of rock's great showmen.
Albert Goldman, 1988

When Lennon prostrated himself before the Acid Buddha, he destroyed his carefully maintained balance with his partners. The more passive and withdrawn Lennon became, the more active and engaged grew his rival . . . Inevitably, Paul became The Beatles' prime mover.
Albert Goldman, 1988

The twelve songs on *Sergeant Pepper* set a new standard of achievement in popular music. It took only four months to record, at a cost of £100,000. It was so different and stunning to hear at first that when The Beach Boys' Brian Wilson first listened to it, he gave up work on his own forthcoming album, thinking that the quintessential album had already been made.
Peter Brown

Paul is very stingy about credits because he wants to give the impression that he's done it all himself.
Robert Fraser, art dealer, on the Sergeant Pepper *artwork*

I was a hitter. I couldn't express myself and I fought men and hit women. I am a violent man who has learned not to be violent and regrets his violence.
John Lennon, Playboy, *1980*

The split vision of parody, which cherishes and derides his targets in the same breath, had always been characteristic of Lennon's divided and ambivalent mind.
Albert Goldman, 1988

John Lennon had a profound intolerance of children, being too much of a child himself to tolerate any rivals.
Albert Goldman, 1988

The king is always killed by his courtiers, not by his enemies. The king is overfed, overdrugged, overindulged, anything to keep the king tied to his throne. Most people in that position never wake up. They either die mentally or physically or both. And what Yoko did for me, apart from liberating me to be a feminist, was to liberate me from that situation. And that's how The Beatles ended. Not because Yoko split The Beatles, but because she showed me what it was to be Elvis Beatle and to be surrounded by sycophants and slaves who are only interested in keeping the situation as it was. And that's a kind of death.
John Lennon, Newsweek, *1980*

Starting over was always one of the great themes of the life of Lennon. Every time he got a new kick, whether it was LSD, transcendental meditation, or primal therapy, he confidently expected a rebirth.
Albert Goldman, *1988*

Brian reached inside his pocket to get a pen, and Nat noticed a whole row of little pockets that had been tailored into his suit. Brian blithely explained that these were 'pill pockets', and that each one was stocked with a different strength biamphetamine or tranquillizer.
Peter Brown *on Nat Weiss, Epstein's New York lawyer*

When he was confronted by the press after Brian's death, John parroted for public consumption the Maharishi's line: that death was the gateway to a better life. In his heart Lennon felt fear. For Brian had functioned like a mother to John, coddling him, shielding him and getting him out of trouble.
Albert Goldman, *1988*

Paul was mortified by the kitschy female voices and by what Spector had done to one of his prettiest songs, *The Long And Winding Road*, which Klein had earmarked as the album's first single.
Peter Brown *on 1970*

Politics was one of John's ways of struggling with being rich. In a sense, to John, being rich was selling out. He was by instinct part socialist, part right-wing Archie Bunker; to be an indolent, wealthy rock star would have made him feel as guilty as sin.
Peter Brown

I've been here nearly two months now and I miss New York. I miss whatever it is, the people on the street. Even if I'm not on the street, I know they are, and it doesn't close down at ten o'clock. This is a bit like England to me. There are all these famous people around and I wonder what they do all the time. What do they do? The supermarket and that's it. It's terrible.
John Lennon, *in L.A., 1974*

I saw Jerry Lee Lewis for the first time ever a couple of weeks ago and was thrilled out of me mind.
John Lennon

When John arrived in L.A., he found Spector was more out of control
than he was . . . Spector acted flaky and weird all the time, and John's
voice was too laced with brandy. The sessions climaxed one day when
Spector fired a revolver into the ceiling of the control booth. He
disappeared shortly after, taking all of John's tapes with him.
Peter Brown

I'm a groupie, one of the biggest on earth. Rod Stewart! Where is he?
I'd like to meet him.
John Lennon, 1974

Forgive The Beatles; they just didn't know any better. How could they?
What happened to them had not happened to anybody else before
except Elvis, and look what happened to him.
Charles Shaar Murray, 1981

He warned me off Yoko once: 'Look, this is my chick!' Just because he
knew my reputation.
Paul McCartney, 1986

The Lives of John Lennon will doubtless have fans and critics alike howling
with rage. He deals in relentless detail with every stage of Lennon's life,
analysing and probing, till at times it reads like a psychiatric report; he
details the psychotic violence, the drug addiction, the whimsical self-
indulgence and absurd obsession with every sort of spiritual charlatan.
Rosemary Bailey, Time Out, *1988*

The great thing about John Lennon was that he believed in the *truth*! If
people say to me my biography of Lennon is too true, too stark, I'm just
gonna tell them that's the way John Lennon would have wanted it
because John Lennon, man, John Lennon is the greatest endorser of
honesty about life that the rock world has ever produced.
Fundamentally, he wanted it *out*!
Albert Goldman, 1988

The worse the story looks, the more pressure you're under to suppress
it, not to publish it.
Albert Goldman, 1988

Nobody ever disproved one statement I made in the whole book. It was
rock solid truth. That wasn't even the issue. The issue was the tone. That
I'd ridiculed him, that I'd mocked him. I mocked Christ! I was guilty
of blasphemy. Of a terrible desecration of the shrine.
Albert Goldman, 1988

If the young John Lennon – noble savage scouse untouched by silly drugs, silly gurus and silly women – came back today, I doubt if he'd have any time for his defenders, who display the same reverential blind faith he found so repulsive. No, the hand he would shake would be the hand of Professor Goldman . . . A man as gifted, cynical and iconoclastic as himself.
Julie Burchill

He wasn't talking about peace the way a politician would talk about it. He was saying that 'violence is a terrible thing because I'm a violent man', as he said over and over again but nobody listened to him. And 'I have to be active on behalf of the opposite – peace'. Violence was his sin and he was trying to atone.
Albert Goldman, 1988

Goldman is a body-snatcher. John has been assassinated and now he's been crucified.
Cynthia Lennon

He became someone who was very neutralised. He neutralised himself, that's the tragedy of his life. He couldn't transcend his violence. All he could do was suppress it. You know, he could tranquillise himself, but he couldn't transmute himself. I think that's typical of pop stars. They don't get on with life. They keeping wanting to go back and start over again.
Albert Goldman, 1988

John was a great man, at times wild and wacky but deep down a wonderful human being. I urge people to boycott this book.
Paul McCartney

Rock and roll isn't a form of entertainment. It's a culture, a civilisation. It has taken over for the past half-century. There's never been anything like it. And here is a man who was one of the greatest masters of it, who embodies its essence. Aren't we going to learn something about this whole civilisation if we look at its leaders?
Albert Goldman, 1988

He was bored. He had too many choices, too little to do. He had never done a conventional day's work in his life and he had no self-discipline. The rot set in when there was no reason to get up in the morning.
Journalist Maureen Cleave, 1980

McCartney's one of those people who everyone's got too much attitude about. If you see how many lives pop music has destroyed from a fleeting moment's fame, it's kinda remarkable that he's still so fluent. People forget what a good musician the guy is, what a great rock'n'roll singer.
Elvis Costello, 1989

Phil Spector

Phil had been trying to construct this giant wall of sound ever since he got started in the record business, and when he heard me, he knew that my voice was the final brick.
Ronnie Spector

I have to give Phil credit. He loved the way I sang, and he knew exactly what to do with my voice. He knew my range. He knew my pitch. He even knew which words sounded best coming out of my mouth. He knew that *Be My Baby* was the perfect song for me, so he constructed the whole record around my voice from the ground up.
Ronnie Spector

Phil Spector was the first man to see pop as the new natural refuge of the outsider. The place you could make money and cut yourself off from filth and also express whatever you wanted without having to waste half your lifetime looking for breaks.
Nik Cohn, *1968*

Spector, while still in his teens, seemed to comprehend the prole vitality of rock'n'roll that has made it the kind of darling holy beast of intellectuals in the United States, England, and France.
Tom Wolfe, The First Tycoon of Teen, *1965*

He *likes* the music he produces. He writes it himself. He is something new: the first teenage millionaire, the first boy to become a millionaire within America's teenage netherworld.
Tom Wolfe, The First Tycoon of Teen, *1965*

He wasn't so much in any dada-beat-hippie tradition as a pop bowdlerization of Oscar Wilde. Meaning that he was sharp and bitchy, fastidious, vulnerable, and that he was a culture snob, that he had great style and that you always felt he was doomed.
Nik Cohn

I was very comfortable with Phil, and he was very patient with me. But did he work my butt off. That intro – 'When I was a little girl . . .' – I must have sung that 500,000 times.
Tina Turner

There were like 50 guys in the studio – the whole room was just jammed full of musicians. And this went on for weeks. I mean, who knows what this record cost – maybe 20 grand. In those days, you could make five albums for $20,000. And this was just a single – *one side* of a single.
Bob Krasnow, *record executive on* River Deep, Mountain High

When she came in, she was electric. We turned the lights down, just had a couple of sidelights on each wall. And she couldn't swing with the song with all her clothes on, so she took her blouse off and sang it just wearing a bra. What a body! It was unbelievable, the way she moved around.
Larry Levine, *engineer, on Tina and* River Deep

Finally, she says, 'Okay, Phil, one more time.' And she ripped her blouse off and grabbed the microphone, and she gave a performance that . . . I mean, your hair was standing on end. It was like the whole room exploded. I'll never forget that as long as I live, man. It was a magic moment.
Bob Krasnow, *record executive, on Tina and* River Deep

He would bring me into his office and play me 16 different test pressings that only dogs could hear the differences on.
Bob Krasnow, *record executive, on Spector and* River Deep

The trade publications gave *River Deep* mediocre reviews. Everybody had it in for Phil. He'd had, what, 26 straight chart records? So everybody took the opportunity to push him down.
Larry Levine

Early in 1966, he made his best cut, *River Deep, Mountain High* by Ike and Tina Turner, and it failed in America. Very possibly, it was the best pop record of all. It was a total brainstorm – Spector was louder, wilder, more murderous than he'd ever been and Tina Turner matched him, big earth woman, one scream of infinite force. At one time, there's an instrumental chorus and everything thunders, crashes, gets ready

for final dissolution. Tina snarls and wails in the background. Then she screams once, short and half-strangled, and everything goes bang. That's the way the world ends.
Nik Cohn

They wanted me to get out there and take 'em to dinner . . . In England they don't give a shit about nonsense like that.
Phil Spector explains why American DJs buried River Deep *at Number 88.* *(It was Number Three in UK in 1966.)*

That record just never found a home. It was too black for the pop stations, and too pop for the black stations. Nobody gave it a chance.
Tina Turner

A perfect record from start to finish – you couldn't improve on it.
George Harrison

When you bought Phil Spector records you were buying no throwaways but huge frantic outpourings of spite and paranoia, rage and frustration and visioned apocalypse.
Nik Cohn

He's a great singer. Gosh, he's so great. You have no idea how great he is, really, you don't. You have absolutely no comprehension – it's absolutely impossible. I can't tell you why he's so great, but he is. He's sensational. He can do anything with his voice.
Phil Spector on Elvis Presley

I'd do a Dylan opera with him. I'd produce him. You see, he's never been produced. He's always gone into the studio on the strength of his lyrics, and they have sold enough records to cover up everything – all the honesty of his records. But he's never really made a production. He doesn't really have to.
Phil Spector on Bob Dylan

Somebody should be much more forceful. Maybe nobody has the guts, balls or ambition to get in there, but there is no reason unless Dylan didn't want it. But there is a way he could have been made to want it.
Phil Spector

His favourite song is *Like A Rolling Stone* and it stands to reason because that's his grooviest song, as far as songs go. It may not be his grooviest message. It may not be the greatest thing he ever wrote, but I can see

why he gets lots of satisfaction out of it, because rewriting *La Bamba* chord changes is always a lot of fun and anytime you can make a Number One record and rewrite those kind of changes, it is very satisfying.
Phil Spector

Paul McCartney and John Lennon may be the greatest rock and roll singers that we've ever had. They may be the greatest rock and roll singers of the last ten years – they really may be! I mean there's a reason for The Beatles other than the fact that they're like Rogers and Hart, and Hammerstein, Gershwin and all of 'em. They are great, great singers. They can do anything with their voices.
Phil Spector

Phil never came out and said it, but I could tell he didn't like the idea of us spending too much time with The Beatles. I don't think his ego could stand the competition.
Ronnie Spector

Motown, I've said it before: they have invented the Mustang body or the Volkswagen body and there's very little they can do wrong with it. They're gonna keep groovin', but I wouldn't be surprised if they release *one per cent* of what they record. If they release 20 things a month, you can see how much they're recording and how much they don't release. Their studios are goin' 24 hours a day.
Phil Spector

Everybody knows The Beatles were immune. Everybody knows that George Harrison was at The Stones' party the night they got busted, and they let Harrison leave and then they went in and made the bust. It was like the Queen said, 'Leave them alone.'
Phil Spector

I'm sure that when Motown lost Holland, Dozier and Holland they got a little nervous for a while, and then they shoved it right up 'em by making four Number One records in a row with every one of Holland, Dozier and Holland artists, including the ones that were buried like Marvin Gaye.
Phil Spector

I don't consider Motown black – I consider them half and half. Black people making white music.
Phil Spector

It was a bizarre atmosphere. Phil had armed bodyguards around him all the time. There was plenty of wine in the studio, a lot of guns being waved around, bullets on the floor. That was a particular and overt expression of the rock madness. There were other more sinister aspects to it, such as the drugs, but I never really had a drugs problem. My constitution always broke down long before they became a problem. That isn't my story.
Leonard Cohen *on making his 1977 album,* Death Of A Ladies' Man

The session began with Spector making a characteristically dramatic entrance, arriving late and wobbling into the studio atop his lifts, a pistol showing prominently in a shoulder holster. He was followed by a big, middle-aged man with a beard, his minder, George, the only bodyguard in the world whose basic job was to protect other people *against* his employer.
Albert Goldman *on the 1973 John Lennon sessions*

His big stumbling block has been the problem that every major pop success faces and hardly anyone solves: when you've made your million, when you've cut your monsters, when your peak has just been passed, what happens next? What about the 50 years before you die?
Nik Cohn

Soul

The pre-eminent figure of all is Ray Charles, who was the living
embodiment of soul long before it became a dominant factor in pop and
whose primary role in forming the style is unquestioned.
Arnold Shaw, 1969

Aretha Franklin has been different class. Out of all the many people in
this book, she's the only talent I can rave about without making
reservations or schnideries of any kind. Simply, she's magnificent.
She's infinitely the best voice that pop has produced.
Nik Cohn, Awopbopaloobop, *1968*

It's just about impossible to over-estimate how big a figure James
Brown has been . . . Really, he's the final symbol of everything Negroes
can do, of the money they can make, the style they can achieve, the
arrogance they can get away with. More even than Muhammed Ali,
James Brown has been the outlaw, the Stagger Lee of his time.
Nik Cohn

Brown develops a number through a series of crescendoes – mounting
steadily in volume, fervour and drive – until the rising tension demands
the release of shouting and body movement. The physical side of love
has seldom been projected with such excitement and power as Brown
can command.
Arnold Shaw, 1969

Sam Cooke had charm . . . Offstage he was sharp, self-confident, fast
on his feet. He was a close friend of Muhammed Ali, one of the first into
the ring to congratulate him after first beating Sonny Liston. In every
way, he was smart. Too smart for his own good, in fact, because a
woman shot him in a hotel, December 1964, and he died.
Nik Cohn

Redding was an 'ecstasy singer' for whom visual contact added a
mighty dimension. At the Monterey Pop Festival in 1967, he did not
appear until close to one a.m., by which time the audience had heard
enough to make it restless and listless. But he came out stomping,

kicked the band out with four beats, and had the crowd screaming within seconds.
Arnold Shaw, 1969

In person, everything he does is an all-out, powerhouse, total emotional explosion. He may start singing *Try A Little Tenderness* with tenderness, but it always ends up 'sock it to me, baby' . . . He can work listeners into a frenzy more quickly than any nightclub performer of his time.
Ralph J. Gleason on Otis Redding

Smokey is lovely. He sings lead in a perfect woman's soprano, not a falsetto shriek or anything so vulgar, but a finely controlled warble, full of it own small subtleties. Pop's first female impersonator, original prima donna.
Nik Cohn on Smokey Robinson

She has a voice that was finally wasted in The Supremes, a voice with a kind of sleepy snarl in it, or else the pitch and faint breathlessness of a nervous girl singing for dimes. Dancing, she is like a wildly animated clothes-horse hung with quickly-changing gowns and silly hats.
Philip Norman on Diana Ross

First and last, they're professional. They sing the right notes, smile the right smiles and move like three synchronised robots. They're lookers, politely sexy, and they open their big eyes for all the people, show their teeth, even wriggle their shoulders. Pink tongues and false eyelashes; they're cute.
Nik Cohn on The Supremes

Musically The Supremes are about seven years out of date – still they move in unison, utter breathless lyrics, wear untouchable ball-gowns as heavy as chain mail, as garish as fire drawn by a child. In Las Vegas – a city the colour of colliding suns but tasting of scarcely-defrosted prawns – they are a positive revolution of good taste.
Philip Norman

Ike Turner – he wouldn't start to play unless they flew a flag to tell him The Man had paid the money. Ike had a safe built in the trunk of his car. Only thing – the car got stolen!
Wilson Pickett

Barry White is the singer who turned black soul music into a product akin to soggy white blancmange. From Manila to Macclesfield his

voice can be heard, grunting and gasping in a register of emotions from A to B flat, invariably expressing agitation at the prospect of imminent sexual intercourse and yet sounding as if somebody is throttling the vocalist with a pillow.
Philip Norman

Motown has 103 writers under contract, working in pairs, threes or chain-gangs and subject to the strictest editing.
Philip Norman

The beauty of Motown is that it gives great artists something to work with and against.
Jon Landau, Crawdaddy, *1967*

Smokey has been approached by many people. He's been offered a million dollars cash, he's been offered all kinds of deals to leave Motown. And most of the time he calls me up, or someone connected with the company, and tells us about the offer. We all came up in the same area, what is now called the ghetto, and it would be hard for people to put pressure on us to do anything.
Berry Gordy

People don't realise what personal relationships we got – the same that we had in the ghetto. And the white people too, they came from the white ghetto. The same ties. We all started with nothing.
Smokey Robinson

Berry works with a rifle and not with a shotgun, hitting the target in one, not slinging pellets at it, hoping to hit it.
Phil Jones, *Motown sales director*

In the manner of the very greatest rock'n'roll, Sly and the Family Stone made music no one had ever heard before.
Greil Marcus

Sly was a winner. It seemed he had not only won the race, he had made up his own rules. Driving the finest cars, sporting the most sensational clothes, making the biggest deals and the best music, he was shaping the style and ambition of black teenagers all over the country – expanding the old Stagger Lee role of the biggest, baddest man on the block.
Greil Marcus

There's A Riot Goin' On was an exploration and a pronouncement on the state of the nation, Sly's career, his audience, black music, black politics, and a white world.
Greil Marcus

The Rolling Stones

At any rate, The Stones were at the Crawdaddy, peddling stuff about midway between the bedrock Chicago blues of Muddy Waters and the pop-blues of Chuck Berry, and they built themselves a following.
Nik Cohn, 1968

At the Station Hotel, Kew Road, the hip kids throw themselves around to the new 'jungle music' like they never did in the more restrained days of Trad. And the combo they writhe and twist to is called The Rolling Stones. Maybe you've never heard of them – if you live far from London, the odds are you haven't. But, by gad, you will!
Norman Jopling, Record Mirror, *at the Crawdaddy, Richmond, 1962*

The Stones had style and presence and real control. They are my favourite group. They always have been.
Nik Cohn

The Stones weren't pretentious – they were mean and nasty, full-blooded, very tasty, and they beat out the toughest, crudest, most offensive noise any British band had ever made.
Nik Cohn

After two or three years of playing rock'n'roll guitar, I still couldn't play those black blues riffs like Chuck Berry. Eventually I saw Chuck and realised that this man is six-foot-six and his hand is as big as two of mine. A normal guitar looks like a ukelele in his hands.
Keith Richards, 1991

The best thing about The Stones, the most important, was their huge sense of independence, uncompromised.
Nik Cohn, 1968

When I was 13 the first person I really admired was Little Richard.
Mick Jagger, 1974

The protest he leads appeals to the young because it is a protest against growing up into a world seen as cynical, uncaring and unaffectionate.

He offers, to an army of emotional children, the unlimited excitement that adulthood invariably curtails. He can continue to ride this tide only as long as he remains young himself.
Fred Newman, Nova, *1967, on Mick Jagger*

The Stones' music is now very much related to social life in the 1960s, and even specifically to London life.
Alan Beckett, New Left Review, *1967*

Narcissism and arrogance, concisely set out in *Get Off My Cloud*, are the keynotes of most of The Stones' lyrics.
Alan Beckett, New Left Review, *1967*

Under My Thumb, Stupid Girl, Back Street Girl or *Yesterday's Papers* are about sexual exploitation, not narcissism.
Richard Merton, New Left Review, *1967*

It is an astonishing fact that there is virtually not one Jagger-Richards composition which is conventionally about a 'happy' or 'unhappy' personal relationship. Love, jealousy and lament – the substance of 85 per cent of traditional pop music – are missing. Sexual exploitation, mental disintegration and physical immersion are their substitutes.
Richard Merton, New Left Review, *1967*

For most people, the fantasy is driving around in a big car, having all the chicks you want and being able to pay for it. It always has been, still is, and always will be. And anyone who says it isn't is talking bullshit.
Mick Jagger

Britain today is a society stifling for lack of an art that expresses the experience of living in it. Our theatre is a quaint anachronism, our novel is dead, and our cinema a mere obituary of it. Perhaps the only art form which has an authentic expressive vitality in England is pop music. It at least reflects back to us the immediate constituents of experience, even when it does not illuminate them. It is no accident that it is the one product of contemporary British culture which has any international currency.
Richard Merton, New Left Review, *1967*

Lonnie Donegan was great. Because he was the first guy in England, in the Fifties, who came out with a totally original thing. I *know* he copped it from Leadbelly and people like that, but it doesn't matter. I don't

think that's important. We copped our stuff out of the Chicago Fifties blues.
Bill Wyman, 1974

We didn't want to do blues forever, we just wanted to turn people on to other people who were very good and not carry on doing it ourselves. So you could say that we did blues to turn people on, but why they should be turned on by us is unbelievably stupid. I mean, what's the point in listening to us doing *I'm A King Bee* when you can listen to Slim Harpo doing it?
Mick Jagger, 1968

Murray the K gave us *It's All Over Now* which was great because we used to think he was a cunt but he turned us on to something good. It was a great record by the Valentinos but it wasn't a hit.
Mick Jagger, 1968

I think it's completely wrong to get totally fucked up and go out and play. I mean, I disagree fundamentally. The thing for me is to be as straight as possible. I'm not sayin' I have to be completely straight; when I say straight I mean not fucked up in me head. Not that I wouldn't take a beer, or get a bit drunk, but I never went onstage loaded. That is, out of control. Never once. How could I?
Mick Jagger, 1972

I find it very difficult to travel with anyone on tour. Bianca's easier than some people, but I'm just completely alone, on tour. I just have to be on my own.
Mick Jagger, 1972

New York is New York is New York. Till you do it there, it hasn't happened. They are the biggest draw in the history of mankind. Only one other guy ever came close – Gandhi.
Bill Graham, American promoter, 1972

I'm sick of playing places like Madison Square Garden. I want to play some small towns. I'm sick of playing places where everyone in the audience looks as good, or better, than I do.
Keith Richards, 1973

I was one of six kids. My dad was a bricklayer and we always used each other's clothes and all that. Very hard life, didn't have much food, pretty rough time . . . and Charlie was pretty much the same.
Bill Wyman, 1974

Mick and Keith came from a slightly better class. They lived outside London in a town called Dartford, somewhat higher class. Mick better than Keith. Keith, his was a broken home, separated parents. I don't think he ever knew his father.
Bill Wyman, 1974

Mick Jagger is the greatest performer since Nijinsky.
Patti Smith, 1976

Mick Jagger is the perfect pop star. There's nobody more perfect than Jagger. He's rude, he's ugly-attractive, he's brilliant. The Rolling Stones are the perfect pop group – they don't give a shit.
Elton John

Mick Jagger loves to humiliate people, but he was nice to me because he needed the music.
Ry Cooder

Then all at once there was The Rolling Stones. When they did it, they created a whole wide-open space for the music. They said who did it first and how they came by knowin' it . . . They took a lot of what I was doin', but who cares? The Rolling Stones. It took the people from England to hip *my* people – *my* white people – to what they had in their own backyard. That sounds funny, but it's the truth.
Muddy Waters, 1977

I think rock'n'roll is all frivolity – it *should* be about pink satin suits and white socks.
Mick Jagger

Really, The Stones were major liberators: they stirred up a whole new mood of teen arrogance here and the change was reflected in the rise of Mod, in Carnaby Street and Radio Caroline, in Cathy McGowan and The Who, and later, in Twiggy.
Nik Cohn, 1968

Every band is narcissistic – that's the whole trip. They all think they're beautiful, even the ones with the bent noses and the goggly eyes. We

didn't think we were pretty like some bands, but we thought we were bloody good.
Mick Jagger, 1974

Keith was my friend from way back, but he was also close to Brian, which was great for the band. However, there were terrible periods when everyone was against Brian which was stupid, but then on the other hand Brian was a very difficult person to get on with and he didn't help.
Mick Jagger, 1974, on Brian Jones

To me, The Beatles are like the British Supremes. The Stones are down. They're funky, man. They're hard. They're like that as people and their music is them.
Devon, New York supergroupie

I was knocked out. Things seemed to be open all night and everything was so exciting and there was a lot of energy. Also a lot of things made us laugh. We were very unsuccessful at first but we still liked it. You see, we knew that we just had to make it in America. There we were touring all over the place on our own and nobody seemed to know us.
Mick Jagger, 1974

Actually, if you're a musician I think it's very good not to be with anybody and just live on your own. Domesticity is death.
Mick Jagger, 1974

I don't like to stay in one place in the same way as say The Faces or David Bowie who spend an awful long time at home with their old ladies and families.
Mick Jagger, 1974

I never liked *Revolver* very much. I don't like The Beatles. I'm not saying that I never liked anything they did and I'm not saying that they didn't influence me, because it's impossible not to be influenced by them.
Mick Jagger, 1974

Now *Blonde on Blonde* was a good album, I really liked that.
Mick Jagger, 1974

Do you know that Mick, every morning, goes out and runs, exercises, all that scene. He ain't self-destructive in any way at all. He's out there doing sprinting in the morning, outside the hotels when we're on tour.
Bill Wyman, *1974*

People say we're a parody of what we were ten years ago. I doubt very much whether they actually *saw* us ten years ago.
Mick Jagger, *1976*

I always think of The Rolling Stones as a rock'n'roll band, and every time they say a ballad should be the single it worries me.
Mick Jagger, *1976*

Keith is always going on in all these interviews that for him Mick Taylor was difficult, but for *me* he was really great 'cause he was so melodic to follow what I did vocally. Still, it's easier in some ways to work with Woody. He *sings* and loons. Not so introspective. Woody probably makes the band seem more human.
Mick Jagger, *1976*

I don't want audiences to be in awe. I just want them to have a good time. With Woody, the band is more good-timey.
Mick Jagger, *1976*

Mick put on that make-up and he's never taken it off.
Jack Nitzche, *who did soundtrack for the 1970 movie* Performance

It's hard on Mick when outside musicians don't know him well. When he starts playin' he scares the shit out of 'em. He's got a very similar feel on rhythm guitar to me.
Keith Richards, *1976*

It's not lonely for me because the band are my friends. It upsets me to see Rolling Stones casualities but it's not The Stones who destroy people, it's themselves. Nothing is permanent and no one is irreplaceable. You can't expect to work with people *forever*.
Mick Jagger, *1976*

Whatever you do best, carry on doing. You could have said to Picasso at 35, 'You've done your best work – what are you gonna do now?' Singing can be a lifelong career if you want it to be.
Mick Jagger, *1976*

I don't think the band would have lasted this long if we'd been on the road the whole time. We would have gone mad. You've got to have some other interests.
Mick Jagger, 1976

If we never came up with another song that was any good, we'd be finished. The songs are the most important thing. And the second most important thing is just having the energy to go out and do it. Just having the energy to go out and play as good as you did five years ago.
Keith Richards, 1976

I don't think that Mick needs to be so conscious of what the rest of the rock hierarchy are doing, ya know? Jagger always wants to know what everyone else is doing. Sometimes I get the feeling he measures himself against others.
Keith Richards, 1976

I've been asked if this is the last tour since I was 19 years old.
Mick Jagger

Woody, never the most tuneful lead guitarist, has as little control of his instrument as a man with a pneumatic drill. Richards, bent almost double under Jagger's ballet leaps, often constructs barely half of some essential driving chord. As mistakes continue, the roar from the stadium becomes subdued. Philadelphia has realised it is being used for a two-day tuning-up session.
Philip Norman, 1981

I think Mick underestimated how much he needs The Stones in order to make a good record. A band like The Rolling Stones you can't buy in a moment. You find a lot of guys who think they can pull it off, but *I* still don't know what the chemistry of The Stones is.
Keith Richards

Rock'n'roll is the rhythm of our generation. It's the epitome of the kind of rhythm our generation grew up with, it is very natural to them. As long as this generation carries on, rock'n'roll will live with it. But now there's a new generation and it's searching for its own rhythm. Each generation has its own rhythm. Our parents had swing, we had rock and the kids of today are taking our stuff and interpreting it for their time and for their feeling of life. We'll see where it takes us. Now,

sadly, they've got typewriter rhythms. People pushing buttons with fingers. But maybe that's the feeling this generation has.
Keith Richards, *1991*

Every time we go out onstage, I always think to myself: This time, the really young kids won't have bothered to come and see us. But there they are, every time.
Bill Wyman

I heard Muddy Waters play six months before he died and he was as powerful and strong as ever. So I say, good, let's find out. It's an uncharted area now for a rock'n'roll band to go on this far. I'm looking forward to it – there's a sort of Columbus feel about it.
Keith Richards, *1991*

Keith Richards is the kind of person that sometimes gives the impression that he's in a world of his own over at the other side of the room, but he's actually very wide awake. He's a man with all the infamy and fortune anyone could want and it all means very little to him. The music is the all-important thing to him. Whether you like or dislike him isn't really the point. The important thing is that he hasn't taken the bait and been middle-classed out like so many others.
Bono, *1986*

When I was 11 The Stones was the first album I ever bought, *Sticky Fingers*. And they're the greatest rock'n'roll band of all time and they always will be. No one can get near them. These acts now who might be selling millions more albums don't have the same significance as The Stones. U2 and Springsteen, it's pomp rock, it's pre-punk pomposity as far as I can make out. I'll be very unpopular for saying so, but I think it's a bit of an embarrassment to see somebody taking themselves so seriously.
Mick Hucknall, *1989*

Keith Richards does it better than anyone else in the world. He understands the history of music, he knows his shit.
Mick Hucknall, *1989*

I'm a true Brit – I could never live in America. It's too plastic and everyone's racing after the dollar. When I lived in France all I did was import things from England – videos, music, newspapers and food like Branston Pickle and Birds custard.
Bill Wyman, *1989*

When my youngest daughter was born, the doctor who delivered her came up to me in the dark, right after the birth, and held up five Stones albums for me to sign. It's a crazy world.
Keith Richards, *1991*

I hope to be half as cool as The Stones for half as long.
Jon Bon Jovi, *1989*

Bob Dylan

I was born with death around me. I was raised in a town that was dying. There weren't no need for that town to die.
Bob Dylan, *1964, on Hibbing, Minnesota*

I started writing songs after I heard Hank Williams.
Bob Dylan, *1965*

Bob was reading Steinbeck now, and he could see, in the sadness of the small, unfulfilled, powerless lives in the remote North Country, how the great dream had gone sour at its margins.
Richard Williams, Bob Dylan, A Man Called Alias, *1992*

Bob was pretty serious about his band, and they practised a lot. It was all a blues sound then. Bob sang and played the piano, and he used to practise with the band in garages all round the neighbourhood. Nobody liked their music much, least of all Bob's voice.
Echo Hellstrom, *Dylan's first serious girlfriend*

Bob was sort of oblivious to the whole fact that people were not turned on by his music. He lived in his own world, and it didn't bother him. There was this cat, playing like they were clapping, when they were really booing.
Echo Hellstrom

I thought *Bound For Glory* was the first *On The Road* and of course it changed my life like it changed everyone else's.
Bob Dylan *on Woody Guthrie's autobiography*

I was completely taken over by him. He was like a guide.
Bob Dylan *on Guthrie*

It was competitive. He had like 20 little girl fans and I didn't so I was pissed at him. I didn't particularly dig his imitation of Jack Elliot or Woody Guthrie. I thought, okay, anybody can get up and do that. He was sincere about it, so he carried it off. That's why he made it, because he was sincere about whatever he tried.
Roger McGuinn *in Greenwich Village, New York*

I was just a Jewish kid from Queens. Paxton came from Oklahoma. Dylan was from Minnesota. I was simply not from far enough away to make it in the Village. But when I was here I was strange because I was American.
Paul Simon, *1986, on his British folkie period, 1963-65*

Mr Hammond asked me if I wanted to sing any of them over again and I said no. I can't see myself singing the same song twice in a row. That's terrible.
Bob Dylan, *1962, on his 1961 debut album*

He seemed very small and very young. I was older by six months and I felt like his mother.
Joan Baez *on meeting Bob Dylan in New York in 1961*

I was falling in love. We sat in our room being interviewed about our respective careers. Maybe that afternoon was the closest I ever felt to Bob: his eyes were as old as God, and he was fragile as a winter leaf.
Joan Baez *on Dylan in 1961*

I knew that when I got into folk music it was more of a serious type thing. The songs were filled with more despair, more sadness, more triumph, more faith in the supernatural, much deeper feelings . . . Life is full of complexities, and rock and roll didn't reflect that.
Bob Dylan

Bob Dylan rode in on a wave of bullshit publicity – half his own and half the copywriters at Columbia's house organ – about how he shared 'Woody Guthrie's vision of a free, loving people', how he used to talk in a drawl without the *g*'s on the ends of participles, how he was a scruffy intinerant roving around with a roundhole guitar slung over his shoulder, and all that. And all the while he was just a nice Jewish kid from middle-class Minnesota, caught up in the then-big folk punk fad . . . He had sat there with peach fuzz on his chin, singing like a hardened Negro loner about cold death.
Nick Tosches, The Punk Muse

Nothing could have spoken better for our generation than *The Times They Are A-Changin'*. The civil rights movement was in full bloom, and the war which would tear this nation asunder, divide, wound, and irreparably scar millions upon millions of people was moving towards us like a mighty storm.
Joan Baez, A Voice To Sing With, *1988*

I play all the folk songs with a rock and roll attitude. This is what made me different and allowed me to cut through all the mess and be heard.
Bob Dylan

If Mersey was pop's puberty, Bob Dylan was its political coming of age. There were previous protesters, the Seegers and Baezs who taught us that the world outside was weeping, but it was Dylan who taught us to weep inside ourselves.
Richard Neville, Playpower, *1970*

Dylan was, like many young people who admired him, a disturbed, unconventional, rebellious and confused internal exile from an affluence he could have had, but did not want.
Lawrence Goldman, Studies on the Left, *1968*

The creative brilliance of Dylan's writing and his profound sourness of delivery was the first sign that popular music was transcending its commercial situation.
Jeff Nuttall, Bomb Culture, *1968*

I think he's grateful for us getting into his material and helping his material become more universally accepted. I think he's grateful. I like him too, man, he's a nice cat. I've had some really interesting times with him, some golden times.
Roger McGuinn, *1972*

Bob spoke bad English in quick startling images, and most of what he saw was for his eyes only.
Joan Baez, A Voice To Sing With, *1988*

He was rarely tender, and seldom reached out to anticipate another's needs, though occasionally he would exhibit a sudden concern for another outlaw, hitch-hiker, or bum, and got out of his way to see them looked after.
Joan Baez, *1988*

Ballad In Plain D was a bitter, vengeful song, clearly excoriating Suze's mother and her older sister, Carla, for their break-up and describing the climactic row that had ended in a scuffle between Dylan and Carla.
Richard Williams, *1992*

That song just went too far.
Suze Rotolo, *girlfriend*

It was a mistake to record it, and I regret it.
Bob Dylan

People have asked me how I felt about those songs that were bitter, like *Ballad In Plain D*, since I inspired some of those, too, yet I never felt hurt by them. I understood what he was doing. It was the end of something and we were both hurt and bitter. His art was his outlet, his exorcism. It was healthy. That was the way he wrote out his life . . . the loving songs, the cynical songs, the political songs.
Suze Rotolo

I met Dylan at this funny little club called The Bear in Chicago just after his first album came out. The liner notes described him as a real hot-shot, you know, a real great guitar player. And I heard the album and it sounded just shitty.
Mike Bloomfield, *guitarist with Butterfield Blues Band*

He came to Chicago and I welcomed the opportunity to go down there and cut him. So I went to see him in the afternoon to talk to him and he was really nice. He was just so nice. I saw him at a few parties and then out of the clear blue sky, he called me on the phone to cut a record which was *Like A Rolling Stone*. So I bought a Fender, a really good guitar, for the first time in my life, without a case, a Telecaster.
Mike Bloomfield, *1968*

I had never been on a professional, big-time session with studio musicians. I didn't know anything. I liked the songs. If you had been there, you would have seen it was a very disorganised, weird scene. Since then I've played on millions of sessions and I realise how really weird that Dylan session was.
Mike Bloomfield, *1968*

Dylan turned to pop for the same reason that painters too were turning, or had turned, to commercial culture. Folk was a dead-end, a kind of academy of song. Pop was to Dylan what cartoons were to Roy

Lichtenstein: loud colours, simplified shapes, a whole idiom to play with. That, and the chance of a better irony, a better attack on society's sentimental heartlessness.
Michael Wood, New Society, *on Dylan's 1968 album*, John Wesley Harding

Dylan has withdrawn from the times. And yet the message of these lyrics, with their lunacy and sadness and their repeated circus images, is clear enough and not that private. If Dylan has withdrawn, if his songs are a crazy circus, it is because the world itself has taken to the sawdust.
Michael Wood

The later songs, when they are not private, are meaner. They are sung to rich girls and helpful liberals. They batter and bewilder them and bring them down, and then they crow. The question has become: *How does it feel?*
Michael Wood

Every night The Stones and The Beatles used to come to the Savoy Hotel and they would play each other their latest recordings and you could see them vying for the top spot as the top British band. Dylan was the one person that both The Stones and The Beatles had great admiration for, so when he held court in one of the hotel rooms, everyone sat and listened.
Dana Gillespie, *girlfriend in London, 1964*

Sometimes I thought I was the only one who saw what was really happening to him. Bob was being spoiled to death on his first tour. He was tacking pictures up on the Savoy walls, ordering heaps of food and letting it pile up around him. Albert was footing the bill, and the room was filled with sycophants who praised each new line that he peeled off the typewriter.
Joan Baez, *1988*

I was doing fine, you know. Singing and playing my guitar. It was a sure thing . . . I was getting very bored with that. I couldn't go out and play like that. I was thinking of quitting . . . I knew what the audience was going to do, how they would react. It was very automatic.
Bob Dylan, *1965*

Dylan had been on a sensation-making tour of mod England where his records were bigger than in his native land. He had been impressed

by The Beatles' beat, as they had been challenged by his kaleidoscopic imagery. And he was taken by The Rolling Stones' unbuttoned eroticism and violent wallop. Out of the interplay came folk rock, which occupied one side of the LP.
Arnold Shaw on Bringing It All Back Home, *1965*

Part of his genius – a word not to be used lightly – is certainly his capacity to always remain one step ahead of the game.
Jon Landau, Crawdaddy, *1967*

Bob had the kind of charisma which never really allowed him privacy. Everyone wanted to be the one to get under his skin, to say the clever thing which would make him laugh, to somehow score a point so later on they could think back to that moment and feel special.
Joan Baez, *1988*

He held us all at a distance except for rare moments, which we all sought.
Joan Baez, *1988*

The Chimes of Freedom shows that his love of the majestic, big, epic type of material is an all but permanent side of Bob Dylan. How many artists would come right out and say they are singing for 'every hung-up person in the whole wide universe'?
Jon Landau, Crawdaddy, *1967*

Dylan came out and it was obvious that he was stoned, bobbing around the stage, very Chaplinesque actually.
Liam Clancy, *film-maker, on Dylan at Newport*

By today's standards it wasn't very loud, but by those standards of the day it was the loudest thing anybody had ever heard . . . There were arguments between people sitting next to each other. Some people were booing, some people were cheering.
Joe Boyd, *folk producer, on Dylan at Newport*

When the sounds of disapproval could not be heard over the overpowering decibels of screeching electric organ, bass and guitars, the audience took to throwing pillows and other objects on to the stage. Dylan left the platform in tears. Only when the MC gave assurances that Dylan would return with his 'pure' folk instruments was order restored.
Arnold Shaw, *1969, on Dylan at Newport*

There was a big rumour at Newport that I cried when I was booed. I didn't know enough to.
Bob Dylan

He was back in the studio within four days of Newport, and in the interim he had written his own personal message to those who had been so vitriolic in their response, those who 'said they did it because they were old fans'. The song was called *Positively Fourth Street*. It would make *Like A Rolling Stone* sound like *I Wanna Hold Your Hand* and it would be his third hit single of 1965.
Clinton Heylin, Dylan – Behind The Shades, *1991*

Highway 61 reinvented rock and roll in a way perhaps only half a dozen albums have done in the 40-year history of the art.
Clinton Heylin, Dylan – Behind The Shades, *1991*

He didn't direct the music, he just sang the songs and played piano and guitar and it just sort of went on around him. The sound was a matter of pure chance. The producer did not tell people what to play or have a sound in mind, nor did Bob.
Mike Bloomfield, *guitarist on* Highway 61 Revisited

Highway 61 Revisited, released in November 1965, was an expression of a man at odds with his followers, resentful of some, angered by others, and a wanderer once again.
Arnold Shaw, *1969*

It was an artistic challenge to see if great art can be done on a jukebox. And he proved it can.
Allen Ginsberg, *1966*

Keep playing no matter how weird it gets.
Bob Dylan's *advice to his band before electric gig at Forest Hills tennis stadium*

I was at Forest Hills for his first real electric concert, and the response he evoked from those who six months earlier had thought him a semi-deity showed the frightening possibilities Dylan possessed as a 'spokesman for his generation'. The absurd thing of course is the fact that ten months after the hostility and the boos, these same people found themselves standing in line to buy *Blonde on Blonde*. As usual it was just that he was a little bit too far ahead of the game.
Jon Landau, Crawdaddy, *1967*

He changed. I would see him consciously be that cruel, man. I don't understand the game they played, that constant insane sort of sadistic put-down game. Who's king of the hill? Who's on top?
Mike Bloomfield

They booed at Forest Hills because they'd read that they were supposed to.
Al Kooper, *keyboard player*

I don't think Levon could handle people just booing every night. He said, 'I don't want to do this anymore.'
Robbie Robertson *on why drummer Levon Helm quit Dylan's backing group*

The closest I ever got to the sound I hear in my mind was on individual bands in the *Blonde on Blonde* album. It's that thin, that wild mercury sound. It's metallic and bright gold, with whatever that conjures up. That's my particular sound.
Bob Dylan, *1978*

The pressures were unbelievable. They were just something you can't imagine unless you go through them yourself. Man, they hurt so much.
Bob Dylan, *1971, on 1965-66*

Dylan was 25. In just five years he had transformed popular music beyond recognition, making rock and roll capable of saying a great deal more than just a Awopbopaloobop, and had been vilified, glorified, even deified for his trouble.
Clinton Heylin, *1991*

There's something very dangerous, something very frightening about this whole thing now. Dylan is very disturbing. Dylan gets up there and sings great thoughts and great poetry to everybody, and when you say everybody you mean also to neurotics, to immature people, to the lumpen proletariat, to people not in control of themselves.
Phil Ochs, *folk singer, in* Broadside, *folk magazine, 1965*

The Beatles had just released *Sergeant Pepper*, which I didn't like at all. I thought that was a very indulgent album, though the songs on it were real good. I didn't think all that production was necessary, 'cause the Beatles had never done that before.
Bob Dylan, *1978*

They make too much of singers over there. Singers are front-page news.
Bob Dylan *to reporters at Kennedy Airport after 1969 Isle of Wight festival*

I made my way through the empty cans of vegetables, Blimpie
wrappers and coffee grounds, till I came to a whole shitload of rock
newspapers. There was *Rock*, *Stone*, *Melody Maker*, *Circus* etc, and even
an issue of *Crawdaddy*, with one of my articles in it. I was very hurt that
D threw it away instead of treasuring it, sleeping with it under his
pillow, etc, but this confirmed my theory that D followed the rock
criticism scene very closely and was extremely interested in what was
being said about him.
A.J. Weberman, *Dylanologist*

Dylan has completely changed since the time he wrote songs like
Blowin' In The Wind, and going through his garbage was just like going
through his recent poetry. There is nothing of any real value to be
found. Bob is now part of the power structure and is a reactionary force
in rock. This is the result of his having many millions of dollars.
A.J. Weberman

Could Bob Dylan be punching me out? My idol, the guy that wrote all
that great poetry? And a punch to the head convinced me that it was.
So then I thought maybe I'd wrestle him down, calm him down a little.
But that didn't work out 'cause he had spirit on his side. He got me
down on the sidewalk and started banging my head against the
pavement. And then some hippies came along and broke it up.
A.J. Weberman *on being assaulted by Dylan in 1971*

Right up to the moment he stepped on stage I wasn't sure if he was
going to come on . . . Because the night before when we went to
Madison Square Garden he freaked out, he saw all these cameras and
microphones and this huge place. He was saying, 'Hey man, this isn't
my scene. I can't make this . . .'
George Harrison *on the soundcheck before Concert For Bangladesh, 1971*

New York was a heavy place. Woodstock was worse, people living in
trees outside my house, fans trying to batter down my door, cars
following me up dark mountain roads. I needed to lay back for a while,
forget about things, myself included.
Bob Dylan *explains a 1972 sojourn on his Arizona ranch*

My wife got fed up almost immediately. She'd say to me, 'What the hell are we doing here?'
Bob Dylan *on being in Durango, Mexico, filming* Pat Garrett & Billy The Kid *in 1972*

I learned by working in *Pat Garrett* that there is no way you can make a really creative movie in Hollywood. You have to have your own crew and your own people to make a movie your own way.
Bob Dylan, *1978*

I just dropped in to see him one day and wound up staying there for two months . . . Five days a week I used to go up there and I'd just think about it the other two days of the week. I used to be up there from eight o'clock to four. That's all I did for two months.
Bob Dylan *on meeting art teacher Norman Raeben in 1974*

My wife never did understand me ever since that day. That's when our marriage started breaking up. She never knew what I was talking about, what I was thinking about and I couldn't possibly explain it.
Bob Dylan *on his studies with Raeben, 1974*

Blood On The Tracks is more than just an affirmation of his genius. For here Dylan had released an album at least the equal of his masterpieces from the mid-Sixties. No other artist in white rock and roll can be said to have done that.
Clinton Heylin, *1991*

Bob's music really is dependent on catching a moment – they're like snapshots, Polaroids. The first take is gonna be better even if it's got some wrong notes.
Rob Stoner, *bass player on* Desire

For instance, *Isis*, we did a reggae version, we did funk versions, we did the waltzy one, we did the fast metal version . . . he's doing that to keep himself from being bored. Anybody who's gonna complain about that shit shouldn't be on his bus! That's the gig!
Rob Stoner *on the Rolling Thunder Revue*

He seemed to function from the centre of his own thoughts and images, and like a madman he was swallowed up by them. His humour was dry, private and splendid.
Joan Baez, *1988*

On the Rolling Thunder tour, I never missed a night of hearing him. It was the intensity, I guess, and the words.
Joan Baez, *1988*

Bob and Sara were ill-equipped to handle the practical matters of everyday life. I was forever handing them towels, bringing them glasses of water and cups of coffee, lighting their cigarettes, looking after their kids, and trying to get them seated together at dinner tables.
Joan Baez, *1988*

Naturally, I was playing a Mexican whore – the Rolling Thunder women all played whores.
Joan Baez, *1988*

Bobby and Joan Baez were in whiteface and they were going to rescue Hurricane Carter. I had talked to Hurricane on the phone several times and I was *alone* in perceiving that he was a violent person and an opportunist. I thought: Oh my God, we're just a bunch of white patsy liberals. This is a bad person. He's fakin' it . . . Anyway, Hurricane was released and the next day he brutally beat up this woman.
Joni Mitchell, *1988, on boxer Hurricane Carter about whom Bob Dylan wrote the song* Hurricane

I went on the road in '76 to make money for this movie.
Bob Dylan, *1978, on* Renaldo and Clara

Significantly, when talking about the film Dylan referred more often to painters than to film-makers. To him *Renaldo and Clara* was a moving painting.
Clinton Heylin, *1991*

There was a presence in the room that couldn't have been anybody but Jesus. I truly had a born-again experience, if you want to call it that. Jesus put his hand on me. It was a physical thing. I felt it. I felt it all over me. I felt my whole body tremble. The glory of the Lord knocked me down and picked me up.
Bob Dylan *in a Tuscon hotel room, November 1978*

Dylan has written songs that touch into places people have never sung about before. And to me that's tremendously powerful. And also, because he's an old folkie, he sometimes writes a beautiful melody. He doesn't always *sing* it, but it's there.
Jerry Garcia, *1989*

For Dylan, a musician-writer-performer, the realm is aural, explored with voice, guitar, piano, typewriter – a realm of sound with words in it. This is where he works; this is where he makes his discoveries. It's not two separate realms, one of words and their meanings, the other of musical sounds and relationships. It is a single place where a single thing happens.
Paul Williams, Bob Dylan, Performing Artist, *1990*

I can't go home without fear for my safety. I was in such fear of him that I locked doors in the home to protect myself from his violent outbursts and temper tantrums . . . He has struck me in the face, injuring my jaw . . . My five children are greatly disturbed by my husband's behaviour and his bizarre lifestyle.
Sara Dylan

Even Bob Dylan hits his wife.
The Stranglers' **Hugh Cornwell** *defends his sexist lyrics*

Marriage was a failure. Husband and wife was a failure, but father and mother was not a failure . . . I believe in marriage.
Bob Dylan *after his divorce from Sara*

I was with him the night Presley died. It was in August. He really took it very bad. He didn't speak for a couple of days. He was really grieving. He said that if it wasn't for him he would never have gotten started. That he opened the door.
Farida McFree, *girlfriend in 1977*

I went over my whole life. I went over my whole childhood. I didn't talk to anyone for a week after Elvis died. If it wasn't for Elvis and Hank Williams, I wouldn't be doing what I do today.
Bob Dylan, *1978*

For me, none of the songs I've written has really dated. They capture something I've never been able to improve on, whatever their statement is . . . People say they're 'nostalgia', but I don't know what that means really. *A Tale of Two Cities* was written a hundred years ago – is that nostalgia?
Bob Dylan, *1984*

Dylan . . . trusts the accidents and impulses of his 'performing self' more than he trusts his preconceived ideas. The result is a tremendous space for expression.
Paul Williams, Bob Dylan, Performing Artist, *1990*

There's nothing tentative about Dylan onstage. I've seen gigs where the songs have ended in all the wrong places, where it's fallen apart, and it's almost as if, in some perverse way, he gets energy from that chaos.
Stan Lynch, *drummer with Tom Petty & the Heartbreakers*

There's a lot of room for free playing in his songs, which makes everything pretty spontaneous. It's just never the same – that's the only way I can describe it.
Mike Campbell, *Heartbreakers guitarist, 1986*

This is a guy who in performance constantly starts singing a beat or two early or late, forcing his band to scramble to find him. The first few hundred times you might think it was an accident.
Paul Williams, Bob Dylan, Performing Artist, *1990*

He's very hung up on actually being Bob Dylan. He feels he's trapped in his past, and in a way, he is.
Bono

He actually said to me, I don't give a shit who plays bass.
Kenny Aaronson, *1989*

Without G.E. the band have become rudderless, adrift night after night, and presumably with little faith in Captain Bob's ability to steer them through.
Clinton Heylin *on the departure of bandleader-guitarist G.E. Smith, anchorman of the Never Ending tour 1988-90*

Playing with Dylan has become just another gig.
Clinton Heylin, *1991*

It rubs me the wrong way, a camera. It doesn't matter who it is. Someone in my own family could be pointing a camera around. It's a frightening feeling. Cameras make ghosts out of people.
Bob Dylan, *1990*

Already Dylan has sustained his creativity far longer and with more impressive peaks than any of his Sixties' contemporaries. I doubt that we have heard the last great Bob Dylan song.
Clinton Heylin, 1991

The man on stage speaks to us constantly of his inner life; the private man, on the other hand, seldom knows much more than we do about the mystery and power of his public self. When he does have something to say on the subject, he says it in performances (Dylan's interviews, for example, are always performances).
Paul Williams, Bob Dylan, Performing Artist, *1990*

Dylan's true autobiography, as with any artist, is his work, in which he consciously and unconsciouly shares everything that occurs in his inner and outer life.
Paul Williams

The nature of the artist is that he keeps going. The paradox of the audience is that we love him for this, and yet we want him to stop and stay in the place where he touched us last, or most.
Paul Williams

An easy way out would be to say, 'Yeah, it's all behind me, that's it and there's no more.' But you want to say there might be a small chance that something up there will surpass whatever you did. Everybody works in the shadow of what they've previously done. But you have to overcome that.
Bob Dylan, 1989

Throughout Dylan's career we will find that although he has a reputation as a master of words, his mastery is more specifically of performed language – separated from his performance, his words can lose their power and even their meaning.
Paul Williams

I think this inspired him. In his recent concerts he's been doing an acoustic set, and using a little band of just guitar, bass and drums, and people close to him say that since the Wilburys he's started writing really good songs again.
George Harrison, 1988

Even now, though he has been a seasoned rock and roller for more than 20 years, and single-handledly controls his management, crowd, security, and stage personnel with only a word or a scowl, when the lights come on and the crowd roars in anticipation, he manages to find his way onto the stage with his back to the audience, fidgeting with a harmonica or two. When he faces the crowd, he looks as though he'd rather be in a dark parlour playing chess. Perhaps in a sense he is.
Joan Baez, *1988*

Without minimizing Dylan's talents, one must acknowledge the workings of an extremely sharp public relations mind in the shaping of his charisma and influence.
Arnold Shaw, *1969*

Groups

A rock'n'roll group is a banding together of individuals for the purpose of achieving something that none of them can get on their own: money, fame, the right sound, something less easy to put into words.
Greil Marcus

We've always had this example in front of us of The Beatles. They broke up and look what happened. Some good things, but a lot of people were disappointed. Everybody would agree that they were better together.
Mick Jagger, *1976*

Even from the very start we wanted something like the power of The Who and something that was as sensitive as, say, Neil Young.
Bono, *1980*

When Lou and I started the group, there was a basic understanding: it seemed more important to be different than immediately successful, to have a personality of our own, to have arrangements like *Venus in Furs* and to give concerts that were never the same.
John Cale, *1967, on The Velvet Underground*

We used to beat each other's fucking brains out every night of the fucking week years ago, literally, and we're still here now. That shows you we ain't any other group. That's why we're successful. We've got four elements – earth, air, fire and water. D'you know that? Yeah, really! I'm water, John's air, Keith's Leo, or fire, and Pete's Taurus, earth.
Roger Daltrey, *1974*

We're the best of friends, but always fighting. It was there right from the beginning. There has to be creative tension.
Stewart Copeland, *Police drummer, 1985*

For me to sing on stage, the only way I can do it is if I'm really committed to it and if I sense anything less than complete commitment from the others, then I get very antagonistic towards them and occasionally this had led to a bit of a fracas.
Bono, *1987*

We had the same fights we had when we were poor, except 'That's my tomato you're eating!' became 'That's my limousine, get your arse out!'
Alice Cooper

We got a good result with The Police, but we were basically at war with each other for eight years. I still have a good relationship with Andy and Stewart. I still love those guys. Whether we play together again is in the air, but it would be nice.
Sting, *1987*

Now, we're actually mates, but in The Pistols they couldn't stand me. Steve hated me from the moment he heard me sing. He thought my singing was horrible. He wanted a proper singer because he was into The Who and The Small Faces, so every time I left the room Steve and Paul were saying, What a cunt! He's hopeless!
John Lydon, *1992*

I'm really a band animal. I just have no interest whatsoever in Chrissie Hynde at all. And when I'm on stage I think my whole purpose for being there is to make the guitarist look good.
Chrissie Hynde, *1990*

I'm a team player, in anything, music, films. That's why I like to direct my own promos. I like to play in a band. Ray Davies solo would not be The Kinks. There's a relationship in a band, a dynamic you can't reproduce.
Ray Davies, *1989*

We broke up the band after *War*. We literally broke up the band and formed another band with the same name and the same members.
Bono, *1985*

When The Byrds were formed, we wanted to *win*. We wanted a *hit*. It wasn't the money so much, it was The Game of competing with the legendary people like The Stones, The Beatles. They were legends to us. Dylan? No, not so much, because we knew him. We knew he

breathed, shat, sat down, fell down, ate, got drunk – he was real
to us.
David Crosby, *1974*

U2 are probably the hardest working guys I've ever met. They're
always trying to improve what they do, and that's all they care about.
Jimmy Iovine, *producer, 1988*

I was so scared that the record has been so big and we would enter
Kevin and Sharon territory – that we'd attract an audience that is just
into big bands like The Stones and Queen and aren't really a partisan
audience.
Bono, *1987*

The story of Talking Heads is also the story of Tina Weymouth's use of
power – how she got it and how she held on to it when it was
threatened. David Byrne has a lifelong tradition of leaving people
behind; Tina refused to be left.
Jerome Davis, Talking Heads *biography, 1986*

It happens to all bands, not just The Police. You start off as a
democracy and then someone emerges as the leader. It usually ends in
trouble.
Sting, *1985*

We would get through a set, 40 minutes long – just barely – of material
that we had done so many times that we were ready to throw up with it.
We were bored, we were uptight, uncommunicative, we were on an ego
trip, we were defensive.
David Crosby *on his last year in The Byrds*

Roger and Chris drove up in a pair of Porsches and said that I was
crazy, impossible to work with, an egomaniac – all of which is partly
true, I'm sure, sometimes – and I sang shitty, wrote terrible songs,
made horrible sounds, and that they would do much better without me.
Now I'm sure that in the heat of the moment they probably
exaggerated what they thought. But that's what they said. I took it
rather much to heart.
David Crosby, *1970, on how McGuinn and Hillman kicked him out of
The Byrds*

I'm still searching for the ideal group, meaning personality-wise, where nobody's trying to play King of the Mountain. Somewhere, there's one of those groups.
Chris Hillman, *Byrds-Burritos bass player-singer, 1973*

I left The Byrds because they were going to Africa. I told them in advance that I wasn't going, but they didn't believe me. When the time came to leave, I told them that I hadn't been kidding, that I wasn't going to a place that was racist. I'd seen racism all my life in the South. I wasn't going to a place where it was accepted as the norm.
Gram Parsons, *1973*

Paul, I must say, is beginning to come out of the spaceship. I told him personally that if he were going to run the ship I wouldn't want to go. He's beginning to see the uselessness of trying to lead people anywhere. People are asleep and they will always be asleep and that's life. I think he's coming out of his messiah/lead-the-people trip.
Marty Balin *on fellow Jefferson Airplaner Paul Kantner*

The Doors, in their success, did little more than pretend to provoke the imagination. They were wholly and obviously synthetic.
Sandy Pearlman, *rock critic/record producer*

By the third album it was like a meteor distintegrating already. By the time we did *Caravanserai* (1972) I had no band. Everybody was busy with buying clothes or cars or the chicks and all that stuff that goes with fame.
Carlos Santana, *1990*

Really, The Yardbirds were just a bunch of randy bastards. I was 18 at the time. It was really nice. Instead of going out and kicking someone's head in, you could work it out through the music. I wasn't really that good a player, it was just fun to purge all those feelings on the guitar.
Jeff Beck, *1973*

Pete, as far as writing songs goes and coming up with general basic ideas, he's fantastic. But Pete Townshend is not The Who. And I think the first person to admit that will be Pete Townshend. And you've got to realise that. The Who is four people.
Roger Daltrey, *1976*

We were the first band ever to have big 4 × 12 cabinets. I was the first bass player to have two stacks, the first bass player to have two amps. We were the first really loud group.
John Entwhistle, *1974*

I feel that we are meant to be one of the great groups. There's a certain chemistry that was special about The Stones, The Who and The Beatles and I think it's also special about U2.
Bono, *1981*

When it came down to it, we failed because we couldn't resist requests for the hits. Ginger did a drum solo and they thought it was Cream, so we chucked in an old Cream song, then I put in a Traffic song, and the identity of the band was killed stone dead.
Steve Winwood *on Blind Faith*

Moby Grape were headcases, destroyed by CBS. They were the first really massive, massive hype in the world. Only, unfortunately for them, they were also fantastic, so it was this bizarre mixture of the most obscene hype imaginable and the greatest band imaginable. It was a great shame. But the music's there forever, isn't it?
John Butler, *Diesel Park West, 1990*

The appeal of Carter seems to lie in nostalgia for the aftermath of punk, when groups frolicked in the decaying remains of this septic isle, and civilisation appeared to be breathing its last as packs of skinheads stamped on its head . . . Carter score with their acid, comically-twisted lyrics, creating an instant kaleidoscope of rotting suburban hell . . . when you throw in their countless seedy puns, it's like music hall with rabies.
Adam Sweeting *on Carter USM*, 1992 The Love Album

We're less like a successful pop group than any other succesful pop group.
Robert Smith, *The Cure*

Within a year of Woodstock, everything that was honey turned into vinegar within the group. It was kind of like what's happening to U2 just now.
Carlos Santana, *1990*

This hi-wattage trio doesn't seem to belong to Geffen, but this is combative, heavy-hitting rock that thinks on its feet. Slightly Pixies-like, but less whimsical. Big in '92.
Adam Sweeting, *1991, on Nirvana's* Nevermind

I love The Band and Buffalo Springfield. I don't really like anybody contemporary. I think REM are just a shadow of bands from that era. I respect their stance, they're definitely more real than the majority of bands these days, but they don't excite me.
Bap Kennedy, *Energy Orchard, 1992*

I think people liked the naivety of Madness as well because we'd never been in bands before and no one had any preconceived ideas about how it should sound or look.
Suggs, *Madness singer, 1990*

I meet a lot of young bands, and very few of them manage to keep the quality and naivety which made them special. So I try as much as possible not to see what I do as a business, but as an experience, an adventure.
Boy George, *1989*

Meeting George really changed me. I've got wealthy parents, right, so I suppose it's a corny thing to say, but I was a middle-class angry young man, and I didn't really know what I wanted to do. But meeting George changed me. He was really wild, and I was quite conservative, and we balanced each other out perfectly.
Jon Moss, *Culture Club drummer*

I went straight from college into the band. I was a nobody, then I was successful. It was not being able to grow. Judy Garland is an extreme example of somebody who wasn't able to grow up properly.
Ray Davies, *1989*

The Wilburys remind you of good old Carl Perkins tunes and Bob Dylan tunes. It's like a pastiche, a montage of all the good bits you remember.
George Harrison, *1988*

Tina Weymouth was an admiral's daughter; her husband, Heads drummer Chris Frantz, a general's son. The dichotomy in Talking Heads was between the all-American, success-orientated values of the couple's tradition and the art-for-art's-sake, politically liberal

background shared by Byrne and keyboard player Jerry Harrison.
Weymouth and her husband gave Byrne a practical vehicle through
which to work. It seems very likely that if David Byrne had never met
them, no one would know who David Byrne was.
Jerome Davis, Talking Heads *biography, 1986*

The Byrds, as inexperienced kids not really knowing shit, were given a
fistful of those sidetracks. And we went for them whole hog. We fell for
the oldest, stupidest American piece of programming there is: the
competitive ethic. All of a sudden our time was spent in preening
ourselves rather than playing. Just the fact that you can play guitar
does not make you smart.
David Crosby, 1974

Stills was unnerving everybody with his deranged mush-mouthed
behaviour. Guns and free-base were often visible around but what was
even more disturbing was his deluded insistence about having served in
Vietnam when everybody around him had to gently keep reminding
him that he'd in fact been playing in Buffalo Springfield at the time he
was claiming to have been on special manoeuvres, killing 'gooks'.
Nick Kent, Vox, *1991*

Bon Jovi are a kind of simpleton's version of heavy rock. Their
messages, about love, friendship or life on the road, are big and
generalised. Corny, even.
Adam Sweeting

Our knowledge of roots music was pretty sketchy in the early days. We
grew up on a staple diet of Bowie, The Velvet Underground, Patti
Smith and the post-punk groups, and little did I know at that stage how
things like Iggy Pop and the Stooges were blues taken to an urban
setting.
The Edge, U2, 1988

I felt that we would destroy the myth of the Bunnymen if we carried on.
With a half-decent album, we would have cleaned up in America, but
we all knew it wasn't as good any more and that it wasn't going to be. It
had become a job and we had always prided ourselves on being able to
fight all that, but we just gave up. Although we're lazy sods, the one
thing we'd always had was a burning need to do it and a self-propulsion
that was never too formulated. Even that had gone.
Ian McCulloch, 1989

I've been in at least five different groups since I've been in The Cure.
I've been everything – punk, goth, psychedelic, pop. It was really great
showing that The Cure could make pop singles. Now we've drifted
back to that sort of atmospheric music we did on *Faith*. But the thing
about The Cure is that we exist in isolation. We're not in competition
with anyone. One day I suppose we'll stop. But we'll never be replaced.
Robert Smith, *The Cure, 1989*

What has made The Police different – and ultimately made them rich –
is their determined rejection of all Rock's mythical excess and
megalomania. They are the antithesis of bands who demand that the
backstage quarters be provided with 1804 Napoleon brandy. And if it is
1805 brandy, no one will play a note.
Philip Norman

Most of the bands never realised they were being charged for things like
that. American promoters are the worst. They charge you for
everything in the dressing-room – even the couch you sit on. A really
good tour accountant, like we've got, can protect you from most of it.
When we go on tour, we take our own food. We take our own furniture.
The couch we sit on is ours.
Sting, 1981

When Guns N' Roses released *Appetite For Destruction* in 1987, its rough-
hewn hard rock and violent, hedonistic lyrics set them apart from the
airbrushed, vacuum-packed, post-MTV pop which dominated the
industry. Nine million copies later, the group have yet to substantiate
their vast and noisy reputation.
Adam Sweeting

Where the band used to be chaotic and unfocused, now they've learned
to harness their strengths around Rose's anarchic energy. Without him,
they'd be an old-fashioned hard rock group, obsessed with Zeppelin,
Hendrix and The Stones. But Rose is an alchemising presence, a
suspect device, able to invest the dullest clichés with menace . . . Guns
N' Roses stood an excellent chance of disintegrating into a sick joke.
Instead they've managed to ride the lightning, and have grown in the
process.
Adam Sweeting

I never used to dream about Jimi. But one night I had a dream and Jimi came into the room. I said, 'But you're dead,' and he said, 'It's cool. I just wanted to see you again.'
Noel Redding

Female Singers

I was the only girl who ever married the boss in the music business. Not even Diana Ross married Berry Gordy.
Ronnie Spector

Dolly Parton's just kind of a Southern magnolia blossom that floats on the breeze.
Linda Ronstadt

I'm not offended at all, because I know I'm not a dumb blonde. I also know I'm not blonde.
Dolly Parton

I walked into a local coffeehouse and there was this girl singing 'I had a king in a tenement castle'. I went *What?* Then she sang about two more songs and after I peeled myself off the back of the room I realised I had just fallen in love. So I got involved with Mitchell for about six or eight months. We went back to L.A. and tried to live together. It doesn't work. She shouldn't have an old man.
David Crosby, *1974, on seeing Joni Mitchell in Florida*

I hang my laundry on the line when I write.
Joni Mitchell

I have yet to meet a girl who doesn't feel Joni speaks for her. Most girls think and speak on a fairly simple level, but feel on a deeply complex one.
Paul Williams, *1968*

I have to be honest – the first time I saw Cher, I thought she was a hooker.
Ronnie Spector

Everything got easier when *Nick Of Time* was a hit. I didn't have to tour all the time – instead of crossing the country three times in a year, I could do it just once and hit 15,000 people in one night. It was great. It meant I could have a personal life again.
Bonnie Raitt, *1992*

Back then, we, the musical heroes, for lack of a better word, didn't feel very separated from our audiences. We were all hippies. It's not like now where the musical stars have become like the movie stars of the era before us.
Joni Mitchell, 1988

There were girls like Joni Mitchell at that time who had voices like angels and they were trying to sing funky and I used to think, Joni, don't waste your time. And then there was Janis Joplin, and she had to prove that she was funkier than any guy there ever was – that she could take more drugs, and she could drink more, whereas actually she was a very well-read, very bright, intuitive person, and there she was trying to be ballsy.
Linda Ronstadt, 1990

Now the band was ragged, the music was manic, overblown, most of the time incoherent, they played fast and loud but nothing much went anywhere, it was an anarchic psychedelic jerk-off. But Janis was truly something else. She was *so* tough. She sang like a rock-and-roll banshee and leaped about the stage like a dervish. It was the raunchiest, grittiest, most attacking rhythm-and-blues singing I'd ever heard.
Michael Thomas, Ramparts, *1967*

I don't feel quite free enough in my phrasing. I sing with a more demanding beat, a steady rather than a lilting beat. I don't riff over the band. I try to punctuate the rhythm with my voice. That's why Otis Redding was so great. You can't get away from him. He pounds on you – you can't help but *feel* him.
Janis Joplin

All my life, I just wanted to be a beatnik, meet all the heavies, get stoned, get laid, have a good time. That's all I ever wanted, except I knew I had a good voice and I could always get a couple of beers off of it. All of a sudden someone threw me in this rock'n'roll band – and I decided then and there that was it. I never wanted to do anything else. It was better than it had been with any man, y'know.
Janis Joplin

I was two and a half pounds when I was born, two months premature. My sense of myself has always been as a very small person fighting against a very large world that is maybe interested, maybe not interested.
Suzanne Vega, 1992

That's actually the message behind a lot of my songs – that you must protect those who are weaker than you.
Suzanne Vega, 1992

The most amazing thing about my childhood was that my baby-sitter when I was seven years old was a certain Michael Bolton! We have a good laugh about it now – I seem to recall that he fancied my sister.
Paula Abdul

For a while I was addicted to exercise. I'm careful about that now. You see girls at my gym who are addicted to it – they get very thin and are there all the time.
Belinda Carlisle

My first daughter was born when I was 20, my second when I was 22 and my son when I was 24. I used to clean windows in the morning, clean offices a couple of evenings a week and then knit jumpers for an American woman who had a business in Galway.
Mary Coughlan

Show me somebody that puts out an album every year and I'll show you a man who hasn't got two children and lives at home with them and has to get them up for school every morning. Oh God, what everyone needs in this business is a wife. It must be great. I wish I had a wife.
Chrissie Hynde, 1991

Age doesn't bother me at all. I mean, look at Tanita Tikaram. She's always being slagged off for being so morose, but you kind of are when you're young, you know. When you're 18, Jesus, you're just so depressed and miserable.
Mary Coughlan

In high school, Tina Turner always got straight A's for drama and gym. And she's still getting them.
Charles Shaar Murray, 1988

When I first saw Ike Turner's band I loved the music but I hated the words. I was one of those school people, and Ike was a street person. I was very sporty and into basketball, and he was nightlife and writing about nightlife things, and I couldn't relate to that because I wasn't living it, and I was not interested in singing about that.
Tina Turner, 1988

Most vocalists, you're really only going to get a decent two or three hours. There's so much concentration involved, going over and over and singing it like it's the first time. And Janet dances while she sings, so that uses up a lot of energy too.
Jimmy Jam, *producer, on Janet Jackson*

I'm not a raving loony. I'm a fiery, passionate woman who cares about what is happening in the world.
Sinead O'Connor

At its best, Anita Baker's voice swirls like the smoke unfurling into the spotlight from a bebop saxophonist cigarette in a 45-year-old Herman Leonard photograph. In the overcrowded field of female soul singers, it is an instrument of great beauty and character . . . She is neither interestingly aloof, trusting in the loveliness of her voice, nor genuinely warm. Sometimes, particularly in *You Bring Me Joy* and *Caught Up in Rapture*, she reproduced the magic of her records; more often, unnecessary vocal elaboration ruined her purity of tone and line.
Richard Williams

Tina was one of the most dynamic entertainers of anybody of any race I've ever met. She's electrifying, and very hard to work with.
Little Richard

Janis could scream and squall, just as hard as Tina, but Tina could dance. Janis couldn't. I couldn't. We weren't dancers. Tina is like a female James Brown. She's a mover and she looks good.
Little Richard

I can't relax. I have to be better than the best. Super-everything. And I'm nervous. My husband, Arne, is a mountain climber. He's climbed Everest. And when he asks me if I want to climb I tell him, 'I've already been climbing mountains.' And I have. It's tiring sometimes. It makes you insecure. I'll probably be insecure until the day I die.
Diana Ross

Berry taught me a lot. It was like leaving home. It wasn't like we were these little puppets and he told us what to do. We were young but the style was created by us, not by Berry Gordy, not by the company.
Diana Ross

People don't know about the human part of me that really cares about the world. For instance, I don't know what I feel about wearing my furs anymore. I worked so hard to have a fur coat, and I don't want to wear it anymore, because I'm so wrapped up in the animals. I have real deep thoughts about it, because I care about the world and nature.
Diana Ross

Nico, the poet's lady. Dylan 'discovered' her in Europe and he and Grossman, his manager, urged her to come to New York, where she soon became Andy Warhol's Chelsea Girl-of-the-Year; and French movie stars were known to call that summer, and then Eric Anderson and Timmy Hardin and Leonard Cohen and Jackson Browne and all the fine young men began writing songs *for* her, *about* her.
Tom Nolan

David Bowie

I was a really heavy Mod.
David Bowie on the 17-year-old Davy Jones

Sometimes I don't feel as if I am a person at all. I'm just a collection of
other people's ideas.
David Bowie

David's present image is to come on like a swishy queen, a gorgeously
effeminate boy. He's as camp as a row of tents, with his limp hands and
trolling vocabulary.
Michael Watts, Melody Maker, *1972*

I'm gay, and always have been, even when I was David Jones.
David Bowie, 1972

The performer is strictly a product of the public's imagination. We're
just a reflection of what people want. It's the audience that are fags if
anything.
David Bowie

Ziggy Stardust is excellent, it is true, but it all seems old hat. If David
Bowie is a genius, then we have reduced that term to mean nothing
more than someone who is familiar with relatively exciting
readymakes, is able to execute them competently, interestingly,
intricately. And if this is what genius has become, it may as well be laid
to rest next to our already-lengthy list of 'So what's'.
Dave Marsh, Creem, *1972*

His flamboyant drive for pop-star status has stamped him in many
people's eyes as a naked opportunist and poseur.
Ben Gerson, Rolling Stone, *1973*

I've always studied rock quite analytically. Only small areas of rock –
but the rock that's intrigued me and got me off.
David Bowie, 1973

Maybe I'm not into rock'n'roll. Maybe I just use rock'n'roll. This is what I do. I'm not into rock'n'roll at all.
David Bowie, *1973*

The fans are clustered in the lobby, dazzling in silver, satins, snakeskins, with thick unisex make-up, and there are shrieks and giggles as the commissionaire lumbers heavily forwards.
Anthony Haden-Guest *at the Pierre Hotel, New York, 1975*

Aladdin Sane is a disappointment . . . Before its release Bowie looked like the most important figure to emerge in rock music since 1967; now we'll have to wait and see.
Ken Emerson, Fusion, *1973*

I taught him to exaggerate with his body as well as with his voice, and the importance of looking as well as sounding beautiful. Ever since working with me he's practised that, and in each performance he does his movements are more exquisite.
Lindsay Kemp, Crawdaddy, *1975*

In his latest incarnation, he takes on the form of an interplanetary bisexual tart. Bowie himself has spoken of the need for some 'unabashed prostitution' in rock, and part of the effect of the rouge and mascara, the white satin pyjamas and the bright orange hair, is to symbolise that he's putting himself up for sale.
Ian Hoare

It's not infrequent that I wake up on a chilly morning and wish I was in Kyoto or somewhere and in a Zen monastery. That feeling lasts for well over five or six minutes before I go and have a cigarette and a cup of coffee and (laughs) go for a walk round the block to shake that off.
David Bowie, *1980*

Every real, legitimate actor that I've ever met has told me never to even approach a film unless you know the script is good. If the script isn't any good, then there's no *way* a film is going to be good.
David Bowie, *1980*

It's the most vile piss-pot in the world.
David Bowie *on Los Angeles, 1977*

It's a movie that is so corrupt with a script that is so devious and insidious. It's the scariest movie ever written. You feel a total victim there, and you know someone's got the strings on you.
David Bowie *on Los Angeles, 1977*

The fucking place should be wiped off the face of the earth. To be anything to do with rock and roll and to go and live in Los Angeles is I think just heading for disaster. It really is. Even Brian Eno, who's so adaptable and quite as versatile as I am now living in strange and foreign environments, he couldn't last there more than six weeks. He had to get out. But he was very clever. He got out much earlier than I did.
David Bowie*, 1980*

No other Seventies rock star has represented so much in the fashions and social conduct of the young, or, for that matter, been so over-weeningly ambitious as to want to extend that influence over the cinema and intellectual circles.
Michael Watts*, Melody Maker, 1976*

He is so dominating in teenage culture not only because he knows so many more things than his rivals, but because he understands how to exploit them to stay ahead, if only instinctively.
Michael Watts*, 1976*

Bowie on stage is almost too cerebral for my tastes, and not enough animal, which is where Jagger's appeal really lies.
Michael Watts*, 1976*

Over the last year I've become a businessman. I used to think an artist had to separate himself from business matters, but now I realise you have more artistic freedom if you also keep an eye on business.
David Bowie*, 1976*

The only thing I know I want is to be Prime Minister of England one day.
David Bowie*, 1976*

He also provided the impetus for kids to dye their hair fantasy colours like blue, green, scarlet and purple – colours that human hair has never achieved unaided – to wear clothes based on *Flash Gordon* comics and Thirties movies, to be exactly what they wanted to be and screw reality, Jack!
Charles Shaar Murray*, 1977*

All my travelling is done strictly in the basis of wanting to get my ideas for writing from real events rather than going back to the system from whence it came. I'm very wary of listening to much music.
David Bowie, 1977

I don't live anywhere, I have never got around to getting myself a piece of land, putting up a house on it and saying: This is mine, this is home. If I did that, that would just about ruin everything. I don't think I'd ever write anything again.
David Bowie, 1977

I must have complete freedom from bases. If I ever had anything that resembled a base – like a flat with a long lease or anything – I felt so incredibly trapped.
David Bowie, 1977

I have to pick a city with friction in it. It has to be a city that I don't know how it works. I've got to be at odds with it. As soon as I feel comfortable, I can't write in it any more.
David Bowie, 1979

Each album was fairly successful at illustrating the particular era, or sort of photographing the time I was in. It was like a musical time photograph. I'd like to look back at my albums through the Seventies and think that I had a little set of photographs of time capsules about what each year was like.
David Bowie, 1979

It is Bowie, perhaps more than any other performer, who began the tyranny of style, image and media manipulation which has been the theme of pop music for the past ten years.
Mick Brown, The Sunday Times

The Seventies

I'm different. I've always known I was different, right from the moment I was born.
Marc Bolan

In many ways I never felt like I fitted into all that L.A. lifestyle. I was too much of a fucking yob.
Rod Stewart, *1986*

Bryan Ferry is the only popular music star to have mastered the visual grammar of Jermyn Street, the only one ever to have worn a real tweed jacket.
Peter York, *style guru*

I didn't see him until the last number. Thank God I didn't because at that time I slept and drank Leon Russell. When I saw him, I just stopped. He said, 'Keep on.' I lost my voice during the next day, and he invited me up to his house. I thought he was going to tie me to a chair and say, 'Listen, motherfucker, this is how you play the piano.' But he was so nice. He gave me a gargling potion that I continue to use to this day.
Elton John *at The Troubadour club, 1970*

Marc Bolan is Mark Feld, a Jewish kid escaping from the dead-end streets of Hackney, clear away but still running hard. Gatsby-like, he created himself in his own image. At 13 he appeared in *Town* magazine as Mark the Mod, the neatest dresser in the whole East End, the main man in the amusement arcades with his razor-cut hair, Burton's suit and alligator shoes.
Andrew Weiner, *1972*

Every Saturday he'd watch the rock'n'rollers parading in and out of the Hackney studios for Jack Good's killer TV show of the day, called *Oh Boy:* Gene Vincent, Eddie Cochran, all of them. And then the lead singer with his local skiffle group must have given him an idea or two: that was Helen Shapiro.
Andrew Weiner, *1972, on Marc Bolan*

Bolan's improbable journey from the most esoteric of the esoteric to the very toppermost of the poppermost seems logical when viewed through the lens of hindsight, but if you had said four years ago that Marc Bolan would be the biggest thing in British rock you would have been advised to have a good lie down until you feel better.
Charles Shaar Murray, 1974

Marc Bolan is now England's number one rock'n'roll superstar. The teen and pre-teen girls curl their hair like his and wear tinsel stars, and maybe pin up his picture inside their school desks. Imitation and identification: Bolan is both fantasy lover and androgynous icon. T. Rex tend to give the appearance of a giant puppet show, Marc Bolan is their living doll.
Andrew Weiner, 1972

Enter Bolan, sweaty and grinning. He's stockier than I would have imagined, stubbly, harder looking than that almost frightening androgynous beauty he had on the *Beard of Stars* album cover. With him is B.P. Fallon, known to all as 'Beep', Bolan's right-hand man and 'information-roadie'. The Electric Warrior hugs his parents and begins to circulate.
Charles Shaar Murray, 1974

Bolan has this very hard, dry, precise little voice, his pronunciation almost BBC except for the slang. He sits there like a little jewelled snake, very poised, very elegant, and we talk about Chuck Berry and Bo Diddley and Nik Cohn and Jeff Beck and John Lennon and Phil Spector and Uriah Heep and whether there are wizards in Tooting Bec and Neasden. He's studied his rock and roll for more than 15 years with maniacal devotion.
Charles Shaar Murray, 1974

I'm very erratic, but that's part of art and I consider myself to be an artist, and I don't feel any compunction to be professional if I don't feel like it, or play if I don't want to.
Marc Bolan, 1974

I didn't like Marc Bolan. I had enjoyed talking to him immensely but something in his vibration disagreed with me. He had seemed like a tiny, elegant steamroller, riding over all obstacles, buffeting people with the wind of his passage.
Charles Shaar Murray, 1974

Stylistically, I've always said that we can't be a heavy riff group
because Led Zeppelin are the best in the world. We can't be a blues-
influenced R&B rock and roll group because The Stones are the best in
the world. We can't be a slightly sort of airy-fairy mystical synthesising
abstract freak-out group because Pink Floyd are the best in the world.
And so what's left? And that's what we've always done. We've filled the
gap. We've done what's left.
Ian Anderson, *Jethro Tull singer, 1978*

Alice Cooper is the quintessential American artist of the Seventies. In a
decade when straight America has discovered that it can't trust the
cops, it can't trust the FBI, it can't trust the CIA and it can't even trust
its own goddamn government, it is only fitting that the youth of
America discover that they can't trust rock and roll either.
Charles Shaar Murray, *1974*

Cooper is a master charlatan; indeed, he has elevated charlatanry to a
higher artistic plane than anybody else in rock and roll had ever
dreamed of.
Charles Shaar Murray, *1974*

Lou Reed is the guy that gave dignity and poetry and rock'n'roll to
smack, speed, homosexuality, sadomasochism, murder, misogyny,
stumblebum passivity, and suicide; and then proceeded to belie all his
achievements and return to the mire by turning the whole thing into a
monumental bad joke.
Lester Bangs, Creem, *1975*

Lou learned a lot from Andy, mainly about becoming a successful
public personality by selling your own private quirks to an audience
greedy for more and more geeks.
Lester Bangs, Creem, *1975, on Warhol*

I've been around. I've met all the women, and I'll tell you one thing.
I'm more woman than any of 'em. Just check my tits! I'm a real
woman, because I have love, dependability, I'm good, kind, gentle, and
I've the power to give real love. Why else would you think such a strong
man as David Bowie would be close to me? He's a real man, and I'm a
real woman. Just like Catherine Deneuve.
Iggy Pop, *1979*

I just played tennis for seven hours a day and dieted a lot. Hopefully
I'm going to be the new sylph-like E.J. by the time the American tour

starts. My guitarist Davey's like Bowie – he's got a hollow gut. It makes me sick. I've only got to look at a doughnut and I put on about six pounds.
Elton John, *1974*

The music I make is rock-and-roll-extremely-jollies, where Bowie's is arty-farty. We're miles apart, and there's no comparison.
Rod Stewart, *1986*

I don't mind people writing books as long as they're humorous and there's some truth in them. I wouldn't stop anyone writing a book about me as long as it wasn't too malicious. I think if you're in the public eye, you're fair game.
Rod Stewart, *1986*

I'm gonna give up playing piano. I'm gonna become a rock and roll suicide, take my nasty out and piddle all over the front row, just to get rid of my staid old image.
Elton John, *1974*

He wanted to combine the fastidiousness of art with the sweat of rock and roll music. He explains this in a set speech, then apologises for having delivered it.
Philip Norman *on Bryan Ferry*

Guitarists

The guitar was slowly intoxicating me. Every lyric that left my lips seemed unworthy of the sound that the strings produced behind it, so I sometimes would not even sing, it sounded so good.
Chuck Berry, The Autobiography, *1987*

You're a blues person only when you're playing. But Negro bluesmen live the blues environment, eat soul food. Even hearing them talk can be like hearing the blues. Rock is like a battery that must always go back to blues to get recharged.
Eric Clapton, *1968*

Stevie Wonder's really the only hope when it comes to progressive music these days. I believe he's the best all-round musician, without a doubt. He showed more versatility than The Stones on the American tour.
Jeff Beck, *1973*

We were just getting ready to go on stage when Chas turned up with this black guy. He was very shy, you know, but very self-aware. Jimi got up and he was left-handed for a start so everything was upside down. It was a little astonishing. He went straight into *Killing Floor*, the Howlin' Wolf song. He did just about everything you could think of, but not in a flashy way. Then he walked off and out and my life was never the same again.
Eric Clapton *on Jimi Hendrix*

His courage came from a fantastic conviction that everything he did was correct.
Eric Clapton *on Jimi Hendrix*

The stuff he does onstage, when he does that he's testing the audience. He'll do a lot of things, like fool around with his tongue and play his guitar behind his back and rub it up and down his crotch. And he'll look at the audience, and if they're digging it, he won't like the audience. He'll keep on doing it, putting them on. Play less music. If they don't dig it, then he'll play straight, because he knows he has to.
Eric Clapton, *1967, on Hendrix*

135

When they told me he was dead I felt fucking angry. I felt, shit, he's let me down. I felt betrayed even though it wasn't a conscious decision for him to die. I felt like the loneliest person on earth.
Eric Clapton *on Hendrix*

It was the first time in my life that someone I had known was dead. All these women came to my room and wanted to commit suicide – to throw themselves out of the window. I'm not religious but I went with all these women to church. Then we went to a cocktail bar and we got rotten. I was shook up. I still don't like to think about it.
Noel Redding *on Hendrix*

Buddy and I flipped out over Jimi Hendrix so bad that we followed him like a couple of groupies. I was just trying to learn how to play the guitar like he did, man.
Steve Stills, 1974

I could never get him to sit down with a good rhythm section. But one time we did out at my beach house at Malibu. We played 15 hours straight, we didn't stop. And I think we must have made up 20 rock'n'roll songs. Bruce Palmer was there and Buddy Miles and me.
Steve Stills *on Hendrix*

I've been the most obnoxious superstar, arrogant . . . I'm still arrogant. I can be an absolute bastard . . . I've gotten all carried away with myself, being a rich man at 25. Sometimes it's difficult to deal with.
Steve Stills

Good musician, but bloody obnoxious. He makes more enemies than friends.
Bill Wyman, *1974, on Steve Stills*

I had to go and see what they looked like right after I got the *Big Pink* album, so I went up to Woodstock and visited, and they turned out to be great people, *incredibly* great people, very intelligent, very tight. And I was in awe of them ever since.
Eric Clapton, *1978, on The Band*

Page was going with us from city to city, as a friend more than anything else. But I could tell he was taking things in, seeing just what kinds of reactions we were getting and where we were getting them. He was already turning into a real businessman. Led Zeppelin, I guess, was beginning to take form in his mind at that point. It's fine that he's

where he is today, because I think that's what he really wanted all along. But I could never be that way. He's so boxed in with Zeppelin, the whole group is, and they can never get out of it. In that sense, I suppose I feel sorry for him.
Jeff Beck, 1976, on his first US tour in 1968

To me, the best formula is one where what you're playing is in no way beneath you but at the same time keeps you and your audience on its toes. Most performers just turn things out to be consumed and digested.
Jeff Beck, 1976

The only pushing I had to do at the rehearsals was of Steve Winwood. He came the first day, played beautifully and Eric was absolutely inspired to have him around. Everybody was. He was an important catalyst. Second day, he didn't come.
Pete Townshend organises Clapton's Rainbow comeback, 1973

We stood in the wings and watched him and *whispered* to each other. It was really good. And you should see his guitar – it's unbelievable. It's got no back on it. It's an old acoustic with about eight pick-ups – and they all work – and he gets the most amazing combination of sounds out of it. He can get a wah-wah without using a pedal, for instance. He's a real genius with electronics.
Eric Clapton, 1978, on seeing J.J. Cale at the New Victoria Theatre, London

What he's doing is what I've desperately wanted to do, which is to age with dignity in this business.
Pete Townsend on Eric Clapton, 1985

I don't mind being thought of as a moody bastard.
Ritchie Blackmore of Deep Purple, 1975

I must be turned on by an audience. In other words, I like to show off. Whenever I get out and play the guitar, I know that I'm good, and I go, 'Right, I'm the greatest', and it all comes out. When I go into a studio, I think I'm playin' to an engineer and a few other people. It doesn't do anything for me.
Ritchie Blackmore, 1975

I know it sounds very morbid, but if we announce that we had been killed in a plane crash, our records would just sail up.
Ritchie Blackmore, 1975

In college I had a lot of fun because I was just playing without a lot of responsibility and without a lot of status. I was treated as just me. When you become successful you tend to be treated like a star instead of a person.
Joe Walsh, 1975

Hendrix was a genius for about three years, then he went downhill because of drugs.
Ritchie Blackmore, 1975

It probably seems presumptuous to call Eric Clapton's first album in three years one of the most intensely religious recordings I have ever heard. But it happens to be true. *461 Ocean Boulevard* contains some of the sexiest, slinkiest music Clapton's ever played or sung, but it also has some of the most profoundly spiritual imagery in all popular music.
Dave Marsh, Creem, 1974

I did it 'cause I liked Dylan's hair. I went and had my hair curled. Then Jimi came on with curly hair, and his band did it to complete the image, and everybody else did it 'cause they dug Jimi; and other people did it 'cause they dug me, I guess. It became quite a trend in England to have curly hair.
Eric Clapton

His tone is vocal; his ideas are superb; he plays almost exclusively blues – all the lines he plays in the Cream are blues lines. He's a blues guitarist and he's taken blues guitar to its ultimate thing.
Mike Bloomfield, 1968

I still feel protective towards the blues. It's a maligned art form and I get angry when I feel people are taking it too lightly. I go back to the blues because of its rawness. It's got more energy and vitality than anything I can think of.
Eric Clapton, 1990

The Rolling Stones are a really good band but I consider them a boys' band because they don't play men's music. They don't play professional music for men, they play music for young people, and even

with their most intelligent material as a stimulant, they play music for the young.
Mike Bloomfield, 1968

Now here is a young cat, extremely talented. For years, all the Negroes who'd make it into the white market made it through servility, like Fats Domino, a lovable, jolly fat image. Now here's this cat you know – 'I am a super spade man, I am like black and tough. And I will fuck you and rape you and do you in, and I'm bad-assed and weird.'
Mike Bloomfield, 1968, on Jimi Hendrix

One of the things which has impressed me most in life was the Mod movement in England, which was an incredible youthful thing. It was a movement of young people, much bigger than the hippie thing, the underground and all these things. It was an army, a powerful, aggressive army of teenagers with transport.
Pete Townshend, 1968

I always used to work with the thought in my mind that The Who were gonna last precisely another two minutes. If the tax man didn't get us, then our own personality clashes would. I never would have believed that The Who would still be together today and, of course, I'm delighted and love it.
Pete Townshend, 1968

He was in a band whose leader was much richer than him, and the leader had shows of his own and a lovely house and my dad still rents a house, never had a house of his own.
Pete Townshend, 1968, on his dad

Whenever my dad got drunk he'd come up to me and say, 'Look son, you know looks aren't everything' and shit like this. He's getting drunk and he's ashamed of me because I've got a huge nose and he's trying to make me feel good.
Pete Townshend, 1968

It was huge. At that time, it was the reason I did everything. It's the reason I played the guitar – because of my nose. The reason I write songs was because of my nose.
Pete Townshend, 1968

I've often ended up in conversations with people who, if my first words to them were 'Fuck off, I don't want to talk to any little creep like you',

they would have gone. But in fact, because I sat down and talked to them, they ended up telling me that I'm a fool and an idiot and they're going to get a coke. This can happen.
Pete Townshend, *1968*

They certainly do have it easy, don't they? In those days you had to punch it out with your father for the car. Today you ask your father for the car and he says, 'Which one?' In the old days you'd drag your old man out on the lawn and kick shit out of each other and he'd say, 'Be home by midnight' – and you'd be home by midnight. Today, parents won't dare tell you what time to get in. They're frightened you won't come back.
Frank Zappa on kids today, *1968*

Music is always a commentary on society, and certainly the atrocities on stage are quite mild compared to those conducted on our behalf by our government. You can't write a chord ugly enough to say what you want to say sometimes, so you have to rely on a giraffe filled with whipped cream. Also, they didn't know how to listen. Interest spans wane and they need something to help them re-focus.
Frank Zappa, *1968*

There are more clowns than good guys in music. British bands don't play as well as American bands. Rock'n'roll is simply an attitude – you don't have to play the greatest guitar.
Johnny Thunders, *The Heartbreakers*

In this day and age I have trouble telling one guitarist from the other. With Edge I hear three notes and I know it's him.
Robbie Robertson, *1987*

When we started it was hard to get The Edge to play aggressively. He is a gentleman and he plays guitar like a gentleman.
Bono, *1982*

Edge can say more about the struggle in El Salvador with his guitar than the written word.
Bono, *1988*

With James Williamson I was basically into what David calls 'guitar-worship', it's rampant among singers – I can tell without even knowing for sure, that Keith Richards will always have it over Mick Jagger.
Iggy Pop, *1979*

It was the first album I've done completely sober.
***Eric Clapton** 1991, on* Journeyman

His choice of notes was exactly right. He was economical. My
philosophy is just the same.
***Eric Clapton**, 1991, on Miles Davis*

Robert Cray is the finest touch player in the world . . . He can play so
quietly and with such grace it's breathtaking.
***Eric Clapton**, 1991*

Keith Richards is my major influence. When I grew up I listened to
half The Rolling Stones, and half Neil Young. And then a little bit of
Zeppelin thrown in here and there, when I was learning guitar, and a
lot of southern rock guitars, I guess, when I was 13 years old or so.
***Bill Janovitz**, Buffalo Tom, 1992*

We would never sell out – REM, U2 and The Cure certainly haven't
sold out.
***Bill Janovitz**, Buffalo Tom, 1992*

Who knew that this kind of music would ever last this long, with this
kind of edge to it, this kind of angle? This kind of rock, with Nirvana
breaking through, it's unbelievable. So who knows? We just take it as it
comes. We've gotta write music that we're gonna enjoy playing every
night for six weeks in a row on tour. That's what really counts.
***Bill Janovitz**, Buffalo Tom, 1992*

Punk

Music's not something you sit down and write. It's something you feel
– like a punch in the ear.
Pat Collier, *The Vibrators*

Rock isn't art – it's the way ordinary people talk.
Billy Idol, *Generation X*

I hate art. I can't stand it. It's treating something that's supposed to be
good as precious. And it ain't precious. Anyone can make a record.
John Lydon

Sneering, sporting women's clothes, shoes, make-up and hairdos,
contending that they add pizazz to their music, the recently emergent
New York Dolls are classically offensive. Their raw, screaming music
supports the obvious hostility of their stage image.
New York Sunday Times, *1973*

The Ramones are pocket punks, a perfect razor-edged bubblegum
band. They should never make a album. They should make a single
every week, 'cuz they've already got enough songs to last them for the
first six months.
Charles Shaar Murray, NME, *1975*

These people have consciously divorced themselves from us to the point
that what they have to say to us doesn't matter any more. What Mick
Jagger thinks about anything is no longer relevant. What Rod Stewart
thinks isn't relevant. So who needs 'em?
Charles Shaar Murray, *1975*

Punk rock? Oh, I've been at it for years, dear. Actually I saw the Sex
Pistols at the 100 Club and thought they were pretty good. Well, not
good, but y'know, they could be.
Mick Jagger

We all lived on the same block and knew each other since we were kids.
We'd talked about starting a group and one day, after Dee Dee and I

had both lost our regular jobs, we bought some guitars and got together at my house. We tried to figure out what to do; took some records that we liked and tried to play them, but we just couldn't – we weren't good enough. So we decided to try and write our own, real basic, so we could play 'em. We came up with things like *I Don't Care* and *I Don't Wanna Walk Around With You.*
Johnny Ramone, *1978*

It's weird. We were on this talk show in New York and this woman is saying that punk rock started in England and Joey says Well, no, it started in New York and she says Look, I have it right here on this piece of paper that it started in England and my information is never wrong!
Johnny Ramone, *1978*

When we started we wanted some kind of definite anti-glitter look, 'cause that's what was going on then. It's amazing how they've changed punk rock bands into glitter. I mean these clothing stores that sold glitter stuff are now selling the same stuff, but now it's punk fashions.
Johnny Ramone, *1978*

Yes, *Pretty Vacant* was very *tuneful.* Too bloody tuneful, ha ha ha. But he soon went. It was Glen Matlock who created that song from start to finish and he was the one that loved The Beatles and the rest all *hated* The Beatles and so, finally, he had to depart. *Pretty Vacant* was *my* idea, actually, that I stole from Richard Hell because he had a song called *Blank Generation* and he had a very good look with holes in his T-shirt which I thought was very chic and endearing, so I said to The Sex Pistols you have to make a song like *Blank Generation.*
Malcolm McLaren, *1989*

We've had it tough. Since we were the first group doing this, we were like the fall-guys for everybody else. We hadda be like the example. Where The Knack comes out and the next day is the number one group in America. After The Cars broke, people were saying, 'Well, new wave, this is all right', and we started coming into the picture.
Joey Ramone, *1980*

I'm tired of the theory of the noble savage. I'd like to hear punks who could put together a coherent sentence.
Lou Reed

At our soundcheck at Dingwalls, all these kids – Johnny Lydon, Joe Strummer – were there, telling us that we were responsible for turning them on. England was like a freak show, a circus, with the different-coloured hair and all. It was great, but kinda crazy.
Joey Ramone, 1990

That was the beginning of the world explosion in England – and then the world changed. Everything changed. It wasn't just the music. There was a whole new philosophy and attitude. Everything changed drastically for the better – '76–'77 was like '64–'65 and the English Invasion. We put the spirit and guts back into rock'n'roll.
Joey Ramone, 1990

Sooner or later – later actually – a group called The Clash take the stage. They are the kind of garage band who should be speedily returned to their garage, preferably with the motor running, which would undoubtedly be more of a loss to their friends and families than to either rock or roll.
Charles Shaar Murray at the Screen On The Green, September 1976

Any reports that I had heard and that you may have heard about The Pistols being lame and sloppy are completely and utterly full of shit. They play loud, clean and tight, and they don't mess around. They're well into the two-minute-thirty-second powerdrive, though they're a different cup of manic monomania than The Ramones. They have the same air of seething just-about-repressed violence that The Feelgoods have, and watching them gives that same clenched-gut feeling that you get walking through Shepherds Bush just after the pubs shut and you see The Lads hanging out on the corner looking for some action and you wonder whether the action might be you.
Charles Shaar Murray at the Screen

Johnny Rotten knocked his false tooth out on the mike and had the front rows down on their knees amidst the garbage looking for it. He kept bitching about it all through the gig; Iggy wouldn't even have noticed.
Charles Shaar Murray at the Screen ·

I saw The Pistols supporting Eddie & the Hot Rods in about February 1976. The bar at the Marquee just emptied – literally emptied, there was nobody in there. All the business posers came out and watched this teddy-boy in brothel creepers, singing. I remember The Pistols being really loud, and bang in tune! The big thing with punk rock was that it

was never in tune. Well, The Sex Pistols, take it from me, were in tune. They could play. Steve Jones, the big fat slob hamburger guitarist, was good, a powerful sound. I liked The Pistols, but from that punk gradually degenerated, 80 per cent of it was just garbage.
John Butler, *Diesel Park West, 1990*

From autumn '76 to spring '77, I probably spent more time with Malcolm than any other outsider. We spent many long hours talking about this and that, and I found him terribly entertaining. Very, very lively, very inspirational, full of wonderful ideas, crazy ideas. He was a livewire, an extraordinary character with loads of energy and a magnetic personality. He was crazy! He was determined to make something happen.
Stewart Joseph, *1992*

He was a great leader and inspirer of the team that he worked with, the artists, the musicians.
Stewart Joseph, *1992*

The Pistols were never going to last. Malcolm was absolutely clear that they would not last. He never saw them as being a lasting band. We talked a lot about the dinosaur English bands who had lasted for years and years. He was very scornful of The Who, in particular.
Stewart Joseph, *1992*

Glen Matlock was always the odd man out. He was the educated one, the bright boy. Jon Savage is quite accurate in how he sees Matlock's role in the band. He was a middle-class boy, he spoke well. I'd have Glen Matlock round to dinner any time, I wouldn't let any of the other three anywhere near my front door. Glen was a nice kid. He was the one that made sure that the melodies all fitted together, and the songs had the right lines, and had verse-chorus-verse, and so on. Without Glen, I don't think it would have happened.
Stewart Joseph, *1992*

He's very off the wall, and he understands the spontaneity of the moment – priceless. If you can get that moment when you play a song just so in front of a tape machine, you got a million dollars. He understands that. Sandy's just a knob-twiddler. Well, not even that – he oversees others twiddling knobs.
Joe Strummer *compares producers Guy Stevens and Sandy Pearlman*

I answered an ad in *Melody Maker* for a rock and roll bass player, which was all I could do, so I played with Mark Knopfler for a bit. And then we started The Vibrators. The first gig we did as The Vibrators, after five weeks' rehearsal – Eddie the drummer had been playing drums for five weeks – was supporting The Stranglers, and we were abysmal. It was a sit-in at a branch of Hornsey Art School, at which there must have been four people. We got paid a tenner and The Stranglers got 15 quid.
Pat Collier, *now a record producer, 1989*

The third gig we ever did was supporting The Pistols at The 100 Club. Again, it was a fluke. I phoned up Ron Watts every day for three weeks, and eventually he said: Alright, alright, I'll give you a support slot, I've got this gig with The Sex Pistols. And they'd just had that press where they'd trashed Eddie & the Hot Rods gear, and no one wanted to know about The Sex Pistols. He only offered it to me expecting me to say: We don't wanna do that one! But I would take any gig!
Pat Collier, *1989*

Our image was based very heavily on Dr Feelgood. We just played a load of stuff as loud and as fast as we could. And the crowd were really receptive, very friendly, very nice. We went down really, really well. I remember standing in front of the stage waiting for them to come on, and McLaren coming down the stairs with Vivienne Westwood, and she was wearing the first bondage suit I'd ever seen. And I thought, 'Fucking hell! What is that?' It was quite striking.
Pat Collier at *The 100 Club*

They sounded absolutely brilliant. And the performance was stunning. We did three gigs with them and they were really, really good. There weren't very many people there, and they weren't very big, and basically they were trying, they were really trying. The 100 Club's not very big anyway, and it was pretty empty. And there were maybe 20 kids at the front of the stage wearing bits of clothes that made them look like they were from McLaren's shop. And the rest of the punks were just 50 ordinary kids.
Pat Collier, *1989*

The Pistols, everybody could play really well. When they were onstage they weren't virtuosos and haven't gone on to have supergroups, but put them together, they were dynamite. They really were *it*. Johnny Rotten's onstage performance at this early gig, when there must have been 70 people standing there looking at him, and he was down

glowering, looking at them, giving 'em all that classic Johnny Rotten stuff. He wasn't doing it for a video, he was actually doing it. They were one of the most stunning groups I've ever seen.
Pat Collier, *1989*

I played drums with The Clash, I also play the drums. I played on the Anarchy tour, where I was known as Rob Harper, but I never get a mention. Pete Frame did his family tree and put Terry Chimes as the drummer on the Anarchy tour, which pissed me off.
Rob Milne, *1989*

The Pistols, I saw them once before I knew I was gonna be involved with The Clash, and I thought they were great. I was taken along by somebody. There were just wonderful. I was one of the people totally geared to be receptive to that thing, at the time. They were *not* musically incompetent. Glen Matlock was a good solid bass player. The drummer was bloody good. The guitarist was dead solid as well. It was perfect. And then on tour I saw them about 12 times, and the odd rehearsal. They had everything, really. Steve Jones played drums at a soundcheck once, and he was a pretty good drummer as well.
Rob Milne, *1989*

We used to see this unusual-looking character with very short black hair and super-smooth complexion, and I didn't like the look of him at first. Then one day I went round to this other flat on the East Slope where I lived, to visit this girl that I'd taken a fancy to. I walked in and he'd already done the same thing. He'd taken a fancy to her as well. And he was sitting there with a guitar. I forgot all about the girl because he had the same guitar as me, an Epiphone Casino.
Rob Milne, *1989, at Sussex University 1975-76, on Billy Idol*

We found that we had similar interests outside of the current mainstream. He was into Lou Reed and John Lennon, and I was into The Who and John Lennon, so we started a band.
Rob Milne, *1989, on Billy Idol*

He was just starting out as a singer, he had the voice but not the control, really. He was really mad keen on rock music and the whole mythology of it. He loves it, and he really deserves to be where he is today, even though he was from Bromley and very middle-class.
Rob Milne, *1989, on Billy Idol*

We did a few gigs on the campus and it went down well, although the tapes I have indicate that it was the worst of the three bands that I was in at the time. It went down better than the others, partly because of the choice of material, and partly because of his frontmanship. He was always kinda confident. He was 19 at the time, and I was his mentor. He used to affectionally call me 'You old cunt', because I was 26. And after we did our first gig at the university he turned round and shook my hand and said 'Thank you – thanks for getting me my first gig.'
Rob Milne, *1989, on Billy Idol*

After a while I realised that he was on to the scene. He had been friends with Siouxsie and Steve, who later formed Siouxsie and the Banshees. Those two came down to see us play at the university before the summer of '76. He already knew about the burgeoning Sex Pistols situation through Siouxsie, and from the first time I saw him he wasn't wearing flares, he was hip to that straight away. As that summer came up, we both decided to leave, to do something in punk, even though the general public hadn't heard about it.
Rob Milne, *1989, on Billy Idol*

It was about that time that he realised he had something. It was a combination of playing in that band with me, and the arrival of punk, so his lack of skill and experience wouldn't matter. He suddenly thought: I'm bloody good-looking, I can make it. One day he said, 'Here, I've thought of this great name: Billy Idol!' He thought of that while we were still at university.
Rob Milne, *1989*

Later Billy said The Clash were looking for a drummer, and that I should go for it. This was the autumn of '76, they were getting some press from Caroline Coon, who was going out with Paul Simenon. The women loved Simenon, who I thought was a complete berk. The other two I got on really well with, but Simenon was just thick. But the women loved him, I've never seen anything like it.
Rob Milne, *1989*

So I went along and got that job. They said: This is gonna be the rock and roll tour of the decade, just come on the tour and see what you think. So I went on the tour, most of which was cancelled, acquitted myself to about two-thirds of my capabilities, but still adequately. By that time I'd already been playing about 14 years. There's a violent side to my musicianship sometimes and that suited them, and me, down to the ground, because I was left-wing, and wished I was their

age, although it turns out Strummer's only two years younger than me. That was the best-kept secret of the period.
Rob Milne, *1989 on The Clash*

The time I played with Billy was the first time I played guitar in a band. I was trying to get away from drumming, and most of all my hazy, romantic notions of how pop music was put together were completely burst by being in The Clash. Because they were strong characters, they were going for it. They were saying one thing to the media, but behind the scenes in late '76 they were saying: We want to be the next Rolling Stones.
Rob Milne, *1989*

Joe Strummer, what a personality! Not loud, but forceful – God Almighty! Quote from Mick Jones at the Electric Lady in Manchester: 'Rob! Don't waddle when you walk!' I knew what they were doing, I wasn't a naive teenager, but I'd rather not have the fame than be ordered about, I'd rather not bother. I think it was a mistake, in retrospect, I should have been nicer to them, and hung on.
Rob Milne, *1989*

If all we've achieved is someone wanting my autograph, then we've gone wrong.
Joe Strummer

New Wave

I manage to look so young because I'm mentally retarded.
Debbie Harry

Sadly, Blondie will never be a star simply because she ain't good
enough, but for the time being I hope she's having fun.
Charles Shaar Murray, 1975

Debbie's persona, innocent yet sluttish, arrogant yet waif-like, was
consciously rooted in America's most mystical of all sex objects.
Philip Norman on Blondie

I did identify with Marilyn. But it was more the blonde thing in
general. Blonde hair we equate with glamour, success, desire. It was
just a great hook.
Debbie Harry

Patti Smith has an aura that'd probably show up under ultra-violet
light. She can generate more intensity with a single movement of one
hand than most rock performers can produce in an entire set.
Charles Shaar Murray, 1975

The Feelgoods really started the New Wave, a lot more than most
people seem to think. They were definitely the first New Wave band.
Everybody says it was The Pistols who started it, but I couldn't really
see The Pistols happening without The Feelgoods happening first.
Joe Jackson, 1979

My ultimate vocation in life is to be an irritant.
Elvis Costello

I try to talk in tune. That's what I do, talk in tune.
John Cooper Clarke

I could never imagine a lot of people wanting this ugly geek in glasses
ramming his songs down their throats.
Elvis Costello

We never play in England anyway, 'cause it's not much fun, gigging in England. The television goes off at 11, you can't get anything to eat, it's not much fun, and we really like coming over here. There's always plenty to look at and point at. And the audiences are very good over here for us.
Nick Lowe *in Providence, Rhode Island, with Rockpile, 1979*

The whole middle America, there's a certain look they've got, which is half-length hair, usually a lumberjack sort of shirt – looks as if they work in a car factory or go to school and wish they were a lumberjack. They've got this look about them and it's no fashion, no style, no cool, no rhythm, *nothing!*
Graham Parker, *1979*

It was good fun except old Van is such a miserable old fucker. It's amazing coz he got us on that tour. We were right down there on the list, and it was him who got us on. But d'you know, not once on that tour did he ever just poke his head round the dressing-room door and say, 'All right, fellas?'
Nick Lowe, *1979*

I know he's very shy, and I know a lot of people like that, who find it hard to mix with people, and everything, but the old Rockpile are very nice chaps, very friendly types.
Nick Lowe, *1979*

There's all these kids, 14-year-old kids, and they're out there smokin' grass, the security cops are ignoring them. It's all *passé!* I mean, they all read *High Times* and think they're taking part in a revolution. And they're not!
Graham Parker, *1979*

My relationship with rock and roll is like Lenny Bruce's with modern jazz – I like the clothes and the attitude.
John Cooper Clarke, *1979*

When I first started I did have this idea about you go out and make a record and everyone grooves on it and then you get lots of money and lots of women and then you get really rich. I had all those silly ideas, but it didn't take long to get it knocked out of me. Well, in fact, it did – it took a hell of a long time to get it knocked out of me.
Nick Lowe, *1979*

Since *New Boots And Panties* became 'the working man's *Tubular Bells*', Ian Dury has been adopted as some sort of mascot, as treasured and beloved an emblem as a battered teddy-bear with a ripped ear and scorch marks on its fur.
Charles Shaar Murray, *1979*

I read that Springsteen brought his kid sister and his fokkin' mother onstage with him. Can you imagine what they'd say about me if I brought mothers and sisters onstage at Rats gigs?
Bob Geldof, *1979*

Immortality doesn't bother me. If people have forgotten about *I Don't Like Mondays* two weeks from now, *no problem*.
Bob Geldof, *1979*

What was so good about the Sixties was that we had so many great dressers to copy. Every time I saw Brian Jones with some new trousers I had to get some.
Patti Smith, *1976*

That's the biggest problem with the last 15 years of rock – people claim it's art, and it's not.
Elvis Costello

Bruce came from North Jersey and I came from South Jersey and we were a lot tougher than Bruce. I had my own gang of guys and we used to eat guys like him for breakfast.
Patti Smith *on Springsteen*

Yes and Genesis are as exciting as a used Kleenex.
Nick Lowe

I never set out to be a spokesman for my generation. I'm not qualified. I don't know about much. Most musicians are pretty thick, anyway.
Chrissie Hynde

Sting is very considered in what he says and what he's prepared to reveal. He isn't Mick Jagger, he isn't Jack Nicholson – he doesn't have the ability to be serious about work without being *serious*. It's a great gift that world entertainers develop, to seem to be casual, and he hasn't got that. It's a difficulty he has. He comes over as very, very serious about himself.
Michael Apted, *director of* Bring On The Night *tour movie*

It's difficult, almost ridiculous, making a documentary about someone who is so self-composed and self-aware.
Michael Apted

I think that's fair. I'm pretty serious. I think all of us are struggling for identity, struggling to find out why we're here. Some people are more relaxed and spontaneous about the process of being on camera. I'm not. I like to work things out, I like to be in control.
Sting

New Pop

The New Pop isn't rebellious. It embraces the star system. It conflates art, business and entertainment. It cares more about sales and royalties and the strength of the dollar than anything else and to make matters worse, it isn't the least bit guilty about it.
Dave Rimmer, Like Punk Never Happened, *1985*

If we need one word to sum up the relationship between the media and the New Pop, that word is: integration. Pop stars sell newspapers and boost TV ratings. Television coverage and coverage in the daily papers sell records and, of course, make pop stars jolly famous.
Dave Rimmer

The boys who were destined to be the Sam and Dave of the suburbs had corresponding bloodlines – mothers who were English, fathers who were first-generation immigrants.
Tony Parsons, Bare, *1988*

Adam was the punk who grew up wanting to own or control everything he did. He wrote, sang, recorded and performed all his own material. He designed his own sleeves and directed his own videos. When he revamped his look around *Prince Charming* in the autumn of 1981, he patented the image through the Merchandizing Corporation of America and did his utmost to try and control every last sleeve, badge, T-shirt, poster or sticker bearing his face or his name.
Dave Rimmer on Adam Ant

Wham! worked like crazy to make people think they were lazy. Behind the suntans lay the sweat and toil of self-improvement.
Dave Hill

Wham! wasn't a scream act when I started working for them. They were initially very hip. My job was to make them a scream act. And then we all waited for the nod from George when he made the decision to stop being a scream act. He knew exactly from day one what he wanted to do. The photographers he wanted to use, the radio shows

he wanted to do, who he wanted to represent him, who he didn't, and why.
Garry Farrow, *plugger*

Even George's pals-for-the-day at the Band Aid recording session had to admit that the blow-dry boy wonder sang better than anyone.
Dave Hill

Madness were the clown princes of comprehensive humour.
Dave Hill

You need a *concept* these days, if you're going to get on. Ask Spandau Ballet. They wouldn't have got where they are today without one. Right from the start these youth-culture-obsessive Islington boys defined themselves as an *idea* as much as anything. They fed the outside world a manifesto, a collection of aspirations and principles.
Dave Hill

Jon was analytical; George intuitive. Jon was a bit of a lad; George was as camp as Christmas. And above all, George was the walking, talking, made-up, dressed-up living embodiment of London's underground nightlife. Jon thought the whole scene stank.
Dave Rimmer *on Culture Club*

I need someone to say, 'Right, do this, do that and let's get on with it.' And when I met Jon that's what happened really.
Boy George

As soon as Culture Club had got going, Jon set about organizing the business of the band. He was determined to get it right this time, never again to be an employee.
Dave Rimmer

I had been really burned in the business and I knew all the pitfalls and I really didn't want to make those mistakes again. So I wanted to have complete control without being silly. Like Spandau Ballet. They've got such tight control over everything they don't get anywhere, you know.
Jon Moss

He nearly always appears to be a bright, funny, friendly, down-to-earth and extremely likeable sort of bloke. Which is precisely what he is – about half the time. When he's in a bad mood he's rude, ratty,

intolerant, perfectly vile to everyone around him and so sharp-tongued he can reduce people to tears.
Dave Rimmer *on Boy George*

I'm quite moody. With a little swift expression, I let people know when they're not wanted around. Or I go to my room and lock the door and people know I want to be left alone. Unless it's a good friend, nobody goes into my room. Nobody!
Boy George, *1989*

Duran Duran have become more than just a pop group expensively decored. They are a full-grown tribute to the primary function of the advertising industry, that being to make nothing very much seem like something we must have.
Dave Hill

I've always said I'm lucky to have a job I like and recording is one of the nicest things I do. When I sing, I relax. But I can't sing to order. At every level of my life, I work off other people's vibes and if I feel I'm being pressured, I'm useless.
Boy George, *1989*

I find it hard to switch off, chill right out, so I watch a video in the television room, or call my friends – my phone bill is phenomenal. I have certain people I'm really close to. Not a lot, but I don't think any of us have that many friends we can relate to, to any great degree.
Boy George, *1989*

Younger musicians than The Sex Pistols and their peers, the provincial ex-punks who were to start the Ska revival of the late 1970s, would carry this golden rule with them into the future. The first law of punk was – *you can do it*. Play an instrument – you can do it. Form a band – you can do it. Go onstage – what's stopping you?
Tony Parsons, Bare, *1988*

It knocked our socks off. I wasn't like one of those little old ladies who saw *The Sound of Music* a hundred and forty times – once did the trick. It wasn't just the film, it was everything it triggered – which was modern disco, modern club music. Everything comes from there. There was disco before *Saturday Night Fever*, but after that it all caught fire. It revolutionised dance music. And us.
Andrew Ridgeley *on the movie that inspired Wham!*

I was a terrible dancer but Andrew and I worked out these routines that we could do at school dances. That would have been when I was 14 – I had just got my first contact lenses. I put my contacts in and suddenly realised that I wasn't Quasimodo. I started getting invited to parties.
George Michael

A couple of weeks after meeting Andrew he took me round to George's house. I don't think he was at his most attractive then! But there was a confidence and charm about him that I couldn't believe. I thought – my God, I have met two such nice people.
Shirlie Holliman, Wham! singer-dancer, Bare

I know that I will never have another time like that in my life. To have that friendship with two boys, and just to be able to muck around all the time and not have any worries. It was all so innocent and your only aim was to have fun.
Shirlie Holliman

I was on the dole for six months. I didn't find it depressing. My friends had a lot of free time and I spent most of my time with them. It wasn't depressing being unemployed – not unless it was pissing down with rain and you were standing in the queue thinking hmmm: This *is* the ass end of life.
Andrew Ridgeley

I had a hell of a lot of optimism but I wasn't expecting any kind of explosion. But Andrew was – and he was right.
George Michael

The reason it became as big as it did was because it was based on something real – our friendship. No way could I have done it without Andrew. I can't think of anybody I have met in my life who would have been so perfect in allowing something, which started out as a very naive, joint ambition, to become what was still a huge double act but what was really . . . mine. I've never met anyone who would be strong or generous enough to let that happen. He contributed so much. It was one of those things that just makes you think it was all meant to happen. The luckiest thing that ever happened to me was meeting Andrew. He totally shaped my life. Not just those years, but the whole thing.
George Michael

On The Road

The period between concerts is composed of different, inhospitable twilights. Dinner at dawn; breakfast for lunch; the day beginning in an hotel foyer at tea-time. Girls are still revolving hopelessly in the doors, crying, 'Rod! Rod!'
Philip Norman

We can't stop touring because we like it so much. I believe I'm going nuts at times – but so what?
Ozzie Osbourne, *Black Sabbath, 1973*

The road keeps *everything* good. Mick knows that. I know that. Any musician knows that.
Keith Richards, *1976*

The funny thing about touring is that you rehearse all the wrong things: the music, the stage show. That stuff isn't the problem, it's the other 22 hours of the day. That's the weird part.
Michael Hutchence, *INXS, 1991*

Fran somehow convinced me to take a vacation: the first of my career. She suggested Hawaii be the place as she had long wanted to go there. We went in November of 1965 and stayed three days loafing around. I had never stayed overnight in any city without working and playing music.
Chuck Berry, The Autobiography, *1987*

It's not such a hard lifestyle – staying in the best hotels, you don't have to wake up till the afternoon. It's not exactly a hardship. I can't understand bands who complain about it.
Rod Stewart, *1986*

It's nice that you can go to any country, and all these people have been waiting to see you for six months, they've bought their tickets ages ago. It's quite moving, really. But it's strange when you come back to your little life in London.
Darryl Hunt, *The Pogues, 1991*

I hate touring. It's so brainless. You just get bored. Even if you partied every night you'd still get bored.
Culture Club's drummer **Jon Moss** *in Japan*

One of the papers said what a sad existence I must have, that I don't have a social life. But I do have a social life. Our floor in the hotel is like a little street in suburbia. We all pop in to see each other and have a cup of tea. It's just like when I was living in a squat, only now I make a lot more money.
Boy George *in Japan*

The fans here are so sweet. In America, it's horrible, you know. They come up to you and go: 'Suck your dick?' It's disgusting.
Jon Moss *in Japan*

Every other city I'd been to in me life, whether it was Nijmegen or Zurich, there was a brick somewhere that was a link with Liverpool. But in Hollywood, everything's purple or soddin' pink, and I'm not a big palm tree fan either. But I've realised now it's just a plane-ride away. You can spend three days there and fly home. I remember we played in Chicago, and U2 came to see us after the show. Bono said: 'You've got to come here for three months next time, three months and you'll crack it.' I couldn't even go to Birkenhead for three months, never mind America.
Ian McCullough, *1992*

I hate waking up in motels in Philadelphia, I'd rather be at home.
George Harrison, *1988*

I don't like being on the road. I like being on stage, but not the road, sitting in a hotel room watching 40 channels at once.
Michael Hutchence, *INXS*

Once we were on a plane heading from Memphis to Atlanta, waiting to take off for a long time. The pilot had switched on the intercom to announce the delay, then had left it on and you could hear him whistling for 45 minutes. We were really drunk and the whistling was driving us crazy, so all of a sudden Townshend jumps up and shouts, 'All right, all right, I'll tell you where the bomb is!' The stewardess overheard him and the plane was delayed. They took us out, searched all our luggage, and detained him for questioning.
John Entwistle, *1974*

To spend five weeks of your life doing that seems a great sacrifice to make. I'd much rather be in the studio working on the next thing. It's part of the work, yeah. It's just the part I don't like.
Bryan Ferry, 1975

The bluff element, which is a huge factor in playing live, gets worse and worse as time goes on but when you're selling out in Melbourne five months in advance or Japan nine months in advance, you've got to ride it and see what happens. We would have great nights but awful nights as well, when we were trying too hard. I mean, how do you practise for one of those gigs?
Jim Kerr, Simple Minds, 1989

It means going into training. Then on the wagon for three months. I knew when I got back onstage, I'd enjoy it. But performing's like sex. You might like it, but you don't want to do it non-stop.
Mick Jagger, 1981

They took 100 musicians around the world – and it worked. We took the message to three million people! I believe in Amnesty and every time they ask me to support them I do. It was great to work with my peers because we rarely meet. You don't play the same city as Peter Gabriel or Bruce Springsteen in the same week, so to actually share the stage, share the airplane, share hotels, share space, share attention, is *great* for all of us. I felt a lot less lonely and isolated. We had a lot in common, and the chemistry was perfect.
Sting

When you do a tour that long your life is on ice . . . Once you've done it for a week, that's all you need to know. You're not going to learn anything new after the first week. Yes, it's great that you can do it for all those people but it's a total sacrifice, you sacrifice everything. Nothing else happens. Only the tour. You put yourself emotionally on ice. You have to. You spend ten months in the company of people who work for you and so you don't get any honesty. You get it to a degree but there aren't enough people around to tell you you're being a wanker. Everyone does what you say.
George Michael

In The Studio

I'm all for perfection as long as it doesn't take more than eight weeks because then it's a bore.
John Lennon, 1974

I remember the pressures it was made under. I remember writing lyrics on the microphone and at £50 an hour that's quite a pressure. Lillywhite was pacing up and down in the studio . . . he coped really well.
Bono *in 1982 on* October

If I want a sound, I usually feel better if I've chased it and killed it, skinned it and cooked it.
Tom Waits

With Eno we rediscovered the spirit of our music and a confidence in ourselves. The emphasis was on the moment in this recording, on the spontaneity. It's like that Irish tradition, the Joyce thing, when you're relaxed you're not inhibited. The recording atmosphere was very relaxed.
Bono *in 1984*

I wouldn't exist as a musician without the tape-recorder. More than anything else, that is the instrument I play.
Brian Eno

When I'm recording I have certain things I have to do. I wet down my hair, I turn my jacket inside out and I undo the first button on my collar. I throw a rock through a window, I tear the head off a doll, I drink a bottle of Scotch and, er, I'm there.
Tom Waits

He's in his natural environment when he's in the studio. He never acts – hey, I'm working, this is important, don't bother me. It's always open arms, come in, listen. He could never go away and record something secretly. He would much rather play it to all his friends, get the feedback.
Andros Georgiou, *friend of George Michael*, Bare

Nine months of listening to The Stones isn't my idea of heaven.
Mick Jagger

I met them when they were doing *Steel Wheels*. I spent a night in the
studio with them when they were doing *Terrifying* and that one that
Keith sings, *Slippin' Away*. That was a turn-on. Chris Kimsey asked me
to go down to meet them, so I did. Rhythm and blues enthusiasts from
Dartford. When I left the studio, my overriding impression was that I'd
been in a room with 48-year-old rhythm and blues enthusiasts from
Dartford. Nothin' more, nothin' less, that was my lasting impression.
The fact that they are who they are is just a by-product of that
enthusiasm.
John Butler, *Diesel Park West, 1990*

Keith was supposed to be there at nine. He got there at two,
chainsmoking. He looked about 140, small guy, very thin, emaciated,
he's got this sort of power from his face. You could be forgiven for
thinking that there's no way that he could play *Come On*, even. He went
out into the studio, picked up a guitar and started boogying on this
blues jam, and it was fantastic, it was like only he plays.
John Butler, *Diesel Park West, 1990*

Press

As long as my picture is on the front page, I don't care what they say about me on page 96.
Mick Jagger

I'm not very good with the press and I don't like my picture in the paper. I've said that I thought I could sing *You Really Got Me* better than Frank Sinatra, and somebody asked: Who is this guy who thinks he can sing better than Sinatra?
Ray Davies, 1989

Most journalists shouldn't have a job. Most papers are a waste of time. A waste of trees. Futile. I'd rather read a tree. You'd even get bowel cancer if you use those papers as toilet roll.
Shane McGowan, The Pogues, 1989

The publicity of my trials came to an end when I was sentenced and the ordeal of interviews dwindled to nil. It was this period of interviews that educated me about reporters . . . When I would read what I was supposed to have said, I was amazed at the difference between the niceness of the person who had asked the questions and the nastiness of the text that had been written. It was about then that I became averse to giving interviews.
Chuck Berry

This was only going to be like the second guitar I'd ever broken, seriously. I went to my manager, Kit Lambert, and I said, 'Can we afford it? Can we afford it? It's for the publicity.' He said, 'Yes we can afford it, if we can get *The Daily Mail*.' I did it and of course *The Daily Mail* didn't buy the photograph and didn't want to know about the story.
Pete Townshend

George is very paranoid about the press. There's a lot of anger in him. I don't know why. He's got his guard up before he begins. But the worst they can say is that he's a boring old fart.
Eric Clapton, 1991, on George Harrison

I saw the inside of the hard journalism business when he'd take me to the office when I was just a kid. I saw how a story could be manipulated. I never trusted it then and I don't trust it now. I never believed 'em when they said I'd made a bad album. Why should I believe 'em when they say I've made a good one?
Neil Young *on his dad, 1990*

If you give one magazine an interview, then the other magazine wants an interview. If you give one to one, then the other one wants one. So pretty soon, you're in the interview business . . . you're just giving interviews.
Bob Dylan, *1969*

If I said I was gonna go down to some bar in San Jose and jam with the piano player, who would want to write that up? Who would want to read that? It doesn't sell.
Van Morrison, *1973*

What sells is bullshit. That's what sells. That's why you've got the magazines. That's why you've got the names. That's why you've got the whole business. It's down to names. Who you know and what sells. It's all business, it's all politics. It has absolutely nothing to do with art . . . or music.
Van Morrison, *1973*

If I changed my name and played with a totally unknown band, it wouldn't be news. But *I* would still be doing it.
Van Morrison, *1973*

A musician's name is not important at all. What it's all about is that you're playing music for people to listen to. To give those people something. It's a process of giving people happiness, sadness . . . whatever, out of the music. The names are secondary.
Van Morrison, *1973*

He was an excellent myth-maker. He blew us up, made us bigger than life. Turned our thing, not into something else, but I'd say he placed a lens in front of it that blew it up.
David Crosby, *1970, on Derek Taylor*

Springsteen will write songs about all the press he's got. He's had more press than any living being who hasn't sold a hundred thousand albums ever. It's amazing. Bruce is bigger than a politician. I haven't

met the guy and I haven't heard his records, so I can't tell you what's going to happen to him.
Lowell George, *1975*

I think the main thing that shits me is that Kylie and I don't wanna be all over taking up valuable space on front pages. There's much more important things.
Michael Hutchence, *INXS, 1990*

At the turn of the Eighties it was time to get me. Chronologically, it's editorial policy: 'We said something nice last time, let's kill her this time.' People are fickle, they want a new star, a new face, a new name. It's a disease of the culture.
Joni Mitchell, *1990*

I take 95 per cent of journalists with a grain of salt because I've done it myself, and I can*not* take most journalists seriously. Because I read, and because I'm a fan, I know what most people like to read. People are *bored* with Lionel Richie going 'I-love-everybody-peace-on-earth-we-are-the-world . . .' *Fuck that!* People *love* bastards. People love a lovable rogue. I'm a fucking rogue! All the world loves a clown, all the world loves a *bastard*.
Terence Trent D'Arby, *1987*

Managers

When I first knew Elvis, he had a million dollars' worth of talent. Now he has a million dollars.
Colonel Tom Parker

Elvis knew he was going big time, and he needed a manager. That was late spring of '55. He was the hottest thing in show business, and still just a scared kid. He got his mother and daddy a nice house, they had three Cadillacs, and no phone. He asked me to be his manager. I told him I didn't know anything about managing. Then Colonel Parker came to town. He knew what he was doing. He didn't talk to Elvis. He went out to the house and told Gladys what he could do for the boy.
Dewey Phillips, *disc jockey on WHBG, Memphis*

I want to manage those four boys. It wouldn't take me more than two half-days a week.
Brian Epstein, *9 November, 1961*

The Decca executives quickly concluded that the Liverpudlian was living on hopeless dreams and empty rhetoric. At one stage, he even had the audacity to suggest that The Beatles would be bigger than Elvis Presley.
Johnny Rogan *in* Starmakers and Svengalis, *1988*

In 1963, Andrew Loog Oldham became The Rolling Stones' manager. Oldham, without doubt, was the most flash personality that British pop has ever had, the most anarchic and obsessive and imaginative hustler of all. Whenever he was good, he was quite magnificent.
Nik Cohn

It's every manager's job to control the media. We really did want to be stars, that's why I don't really regret anything.
Mick Jagger, *1974*

Spector was a very great influence on Andrew. I mean, Andrew was so openly influenced by him that it was disgraceful. Andrew really didn't

have too many original ideas at all, he just nicked – that was Andrew's philosophy.
Mick Jagger, *1974, on Loog Oldham*

As manager, what Oldham did was to take everything implicit in The Stones and blow it up one hundred times. Long-haired and ugly and anarchic as they were, Oldham made them more so, and he turned them into everything parents would most hate, be most frightened by. All the time, he goaded them to be wilder, nastier, fouler in every way, and they were – they swore, sneered, snarled and, deliberately, they came on cretinous.
Nik Cohn, *1968*

By the end of 1963, Brian Epstein was able to look back at a year in which his artistes had dominated the hit parade with an incredible nine number ones, spanning 32 weeks at the top. No manager in British pop history has ever achieved comparable chart supremacy.
Johnny Rogan, *1988*

Inevitably, being so successful, he'd been the butt of much schnidery within the industry and, generally, he'd been rated pretty low. Paraphrased, the party line was that he was really a less-than-averagely shrewd businessman, but he'd gotten lucky one time, very lucky, and he'd happened to be hanging round as The Beatles came by. Also, beyond incompetence, he was meant to be weak, vain and maudlin. Most of this was true. Just the same, I liked him.
Nik Cohn *on Brian Epstein*

Why don't you call it *Queer Jew*?
John Lennon's *suggestion as a title for Brian's autobiography*

Derek was a handsome, clean-shaven fellow who had come to Brian's and The Beatles' attention in 1963 in Southport, when, as the theatre critic of the northern edition of *The Daily Express*, he had blithely kicked down their dressing-room door to ask them a question.
Peter Brown *on Derek Taylor*

Derek was hired for £1,000 plus two per cent royalties, a handsome fee for a journalist who made only £35 a week at his newspaper job and had a wife and three children.
Peter Brown *on Derek Taylor being hired to ghost* A Cellarful of Noise *for Brian Epstein*

In literal terms Brian signed over to Dick James 50 per cent of Lennon-McCartney's publishing fee for nothing. It made Dick wealthy beyond imagination in 18 months.
Peter Brown

Brian found himself deluged by ideas from people who knew what The Beatles should do instead of touring. Many of these people were would-be managers, circling Brian like sharks in the water. The most aggressive of these was a man named Allen Klein. He was a fast-talking, dirty-mouthed man in his early thirties, sloppily dressed and grossly overweight.
Peter Brown *on 1967*

Most of all, John and Yoko were impressed by Klein's true appreciation of John's music. Klein was a true-blooded record business man; he loved his clients and he loved their music. He was able to quote from every song of John's already large body of work. This left John feeling terribly flattered and slightly softheaded, a bit of putty in Klein's hands.
Peter Brown

One day, rather offhandedly, Paul said to Klein, 'Either let me out of my contracts or I'll sue you.' Klein, who had been sued over 40 times before, just laughed at him.
Peter Brown on 1970

His choice of press officers, for example, brilliantly complemented The Beatles' ever-changing public image. In the Cavern days, there was the tough, part-time hustler, Andrew Oldham; the Liverpool to London route was smoothed over by a freelance journalist, Tony Barrow; the Royal Variety performances and Palladium spectaculars ushered in a sophisticated former Royal Navy lieutenant commander, Brian Sommerville; finally, there was the eccentric, sentimental, laid-back, quest-seeking Derek Taylor who, like Brian, loved The Beatles as though they were his own children.
Johnny Rogan

We were all standing in the airport, CSN and myself, and it was agreed by the managers David Geffen and Elliott Roberts, that I should not go because it would be difficult to get me out of there and back to New York for a television show that Monday night. If it happened now I think I would have given them a good argument because it kind of

broke my heart. But I was the girl in the family. 'Daddy' said I couldn't go.
Joni Mitchell *on why she missed Woodstock*

Elliott Roberts is a good dude. And he is not a fair-weather friend, and he is not a bullshitter. However, he is, in his managerial capacity, capable of lying straight-faced to anyone, anytime, ever. But he's a really beautiful cat, he really has a heart and it's plain that he does . . . unless you gotta write a contract with him. In which case you may just not ever want to speak to him again. He not only doesn't give away anything, he's armed robbery in a business deal. And if he doesn't rob you blind he'll send Dave Geffen over – he'll take your whole company. And sell it while you're out to lunch, you know. Those two guys, man, are not kidding.
David Crosby, *1970*

If I'd been managing The Beatles I'd have told them, instead of playing Shea Stadium, let's do a week of dates in the field where Buddy Holly's plane crashed.
Bill Drummond, *manager of The Teardrop Explodes, 1986*

Joe Walsh is an Eagle now, and as such he doesn't speak to the Press.
Irving Azoff

He's Napoleon with a heart.
Don Henley *on Irving Azoff*

There's a strength about him that Elton always needed, and still needs. He's the one who fights battles for Elton. He'll go out in the playground and bash big boys up. He doesn't care. And he'll protect Elton until the last drop of blood is spilt.
John Hall, *boss of Rocket Records, on John Reid*

Offered a glass of champagne instead, Reid threw the contents of the glass at Williams, and stormed out of the room. About ten minutes later – according to subsequent courtroom testimony – he returned to the bar. Sitting there was a woman friend of Williams's, a journalist named Judith Baragwanath, who in forthright antipodean fashion, rebuked Reid for his earlier behaviour. Reid then hit her, knocking her to the floor.
Philip Norman, Elton, *1991, on New Zealand, 1974*

John Reid then intervened, knocking Wheeler down and kicking him as he lay on the floor. To hit one person in the course of a day may be considered unfortunate. To hit two – especially in a foreign country, under a foreign legal system – exceeds even Lady Bracknell's definition of carelessness.
Philip Norman

Elton had been released from police custody, but was distraught at Reid's imprisonment and would not contemplate going on stage without him . . . Mr Justice Mahon accepted that Reid was indispensable to the concert and granted bail on condition he surrendered his passport.
Philip Norman

They looked to me like they would be a great rock band. I've only had to be right once.
U2's **Paul McGuinness**

What has kept us together? Fear of our manager!
Bono, *1987*

They'll play anywhere to anyone. They're prepared to do anything for success!
Miles Copeland, *Police manager*

I never knew a musician who wasn't more concerned about money than I was.
Miles Copeland

If Adam was the first of the artists as businessmen then McLaren was the businessman as artist. He didn't play the guitar, but he did play the media. More interested in an adventure than a career, he was in some respects an awful manager. He just didn't care. No good going to him if you were looking for a future in the pop game. He'd drop you as soon as he got bored.
Dave Rimmer

It was all very easy for Malcolm to sit behind a desk or behind a phone and pontificate, saying We're troublemakers and, We're into violence. I was the sod who had to live the violence on the street, get beaten up. Thank you, Malcolm. Sid hated Malcolm. It was all you could do to stop Sid pummelling him every chance he got.
John Lydon, *1992*

Every time there was an interview, it was Malcolm who was being interviewed, not us. And that wasn't what it was all about. Not for me anyway.
Glen Matlock, I Was A Teenage Sex Pistol, *1990*

Adam was just too *dull* because he was too much of a student. I felt like I was giving him evening classes in how to be a rock'n'roll star. I gave him books on Geronimo and the idea of the white stripe on his face and the pirate look.
Malcolm McLaren, *1989, on Adam Ant*

I tend to look quite favourably on McLaren. He was always an extraordinary ideas person, a creative force. Arguably, you could sit McLaren, for his whacky genius, alongside Phil Spector. I can't think of anybody else who has been so off-the-wall, and so into himself, and his own endless creative energy. His ideas have rolled on, year after year.
Stewart Joseph, *1992*

There's people patting Malcolm McLaren on the head somewhere. He reckons he's turned the world upside down. He fucking hasn't.
Nick Lowe, *1979*

In Australia, where the [capacity of the] biggest building is only about 12,000, we ended up playing ten or 11 nights in Sydney and it was awful. You get a lot of people coming back for the second time and the spontaneity of the show suffers.
Paul McGuinness, *U2*

More than most bands, we take control of the circumstances in which we perform. It's part of the process we apply to most things, of not letting luck, or indeed other people's judgements, control us.
Paul McGuinness, *U2*

I think it is extremely unprofessional. It's full of people who want to pose and lig and be full of their own self-importance. We have tried to give management a more professional status away from the sleazy rip-off Mafia connotations. I am just a member of the team, no more important than the drum roadie or the fan-club secretary. Sure, everyone has to have a captain and I am the one who signs the cheques, but the moment you start to acquire that attitude you go the way of every other rock'n'roll tragedy you've ever seen.
Tom Watkins, *Massive Management, 1988*

The Pet Shop Boys are the two most enjoyable people I've worked with. They know exactly what they want to do, which makes our job a whole lot easier.
Tom Watkins, *1988*

Design is vital to me. I get very upset by what they are doing to the environment. I'm obsessed by the Thirties. I like the Modernist movement just before the war, when people were waking up to the idea that it was commercially feasible to have beautiful lines. I like the idea of a *Daily Mail* ideal home. I like manufacturing. I like mass style. Personally I like clear, clean-cut modernist lines. You could say Bros have modernist haircuts.
Tom Watkins, *1988*

Most managers seem to be thieves. Real no-good rotten fucking bastard thieves.
Lou Reed, *1972*

Rock'n'roll is not just music. You're selling an attitude, too. Take away the attitude and you're just like anyone else. The kids need a sense of adventure and rock'n'roll gives it to them. Wham out the hardest and cruellest lyrics as propaganda, speak the truth as clearly as possible.
Malcom McLaren

If you play a 13,000-seater hall in somewhere like Tallahassee, Florida, they're so glad that you're using their facility that they won't charge any commission on T-shirt sales. But if you play Madison Square Garden the hall can take up to 50 per cent commission so you can end up losing money. It becomes more profitable to play to 13,000 people in Tallahassee than 35,000 people in New York City. We're not in the music business anymore. We're in the commodities business.
Miles Copeland, *The Police*

There was a lot of music on *Private Dancer* which she didn't really like, to be honest, and she'll tell you that herself. But I said: That's the direction we have to go in. I know you want do an AC/DC album, but we're not ready for that yet. If Tina had a choice, she'd do a real hard rock, heavy metal album. I don't mean bang-your-head-against-the-wall stuff, but real good pumping stuff like early AC/DC.
Roger Davies, *Tina Turner's Australian manager*

Tina fell in love with Europe when she toured here, and she wanted to live that way. I don't want this taken the wrong way, and Tina can explain this better than I can, but she's not a typical black person. She's a determined person. If an act had success and had a chip on his shoulder and is bitter, there's not a chance in hell that they're gonna do it again. She wanted this success *desperately*. She wanted to prove to herself that she could do it.
Roger Davies

Sure, we tout our own tickets. When we do a big gig like Elland Road last summer, part of the contract with the promoter is that we get a thousand tickets. About half of them we give away to friends, which is more than £7,500 worth, and the other half – well, I lock them in the safe, but the band come round the office when I'm out and terrorise the staff into handing them over. Then they sell them to the touts.
Nathan McGough, *The Happy Mondays, 1992*

Performance

He seems to attract this gentle adoration in everybody, but you'd need
a sociology degree to work it out.
Jo Slee, *Morrissey's personal assistant*

I've opened for Black Oak Arkansas. I've opened for Brownsville
Station, and I've opened for Sha Na Na. I'm 31 – and I've been playing
in bars since I was 15. And I've faced a lot of audiences that don't give
a *shit* that you're onstage.
Bruce Springsteen, *1981*

If it wasn't for the feeling I get while performing, I think it would have
been impossible for me to have continued as long as I have.
Chuck Berry, The Autobiography

There's nothing like being onstage. You can't put it in words. When the
lights hit you, there's a certain spirit you feel. I don't like coming off!
Michael Jackson

That's one of the best feelings on the market, when you walk up those
steps to the stage. It feels like sparks are flying through you. I get tears
in my eyes and – I know this sound really schmaltzy – but I just want to
give.
Michael Hutchence, *INXS, 1991*

It's a pretty cool feeling going out there and seeing 70,000 smiling faces.
Greatest feeling in the world.
Jon Bon Jovi, *1991*

While he was playing, he accidentally kicked his piano stool over. It got
a terrific reaction from the audience, so, at the next gig, he kicked it
over on purpose.
Publisher Ray Williams *on Elton John supporting Tyrannosaurus Rex at the
Roundhouse, London, 1969*

I can't understand people who say they don't like doing concerts. It's the greatest thing in the world to stand on a stage and see people in the front rows smiling, and know they came to see you.
Elton John, Los Angeles, 1974

We only had to do 20 minutes – and that still used to seem like an hour to me. There were four of us, but you do two and a half hours on your own. How the fuck do you do it?
John Lennon to Elton John, 1973

With its dozen-strong dance troupe, set-piece dialogues, elaborate costumes and multiple sets, including a *Metropolis*-style futurist nightmare, a cathedral, a harem and a Thirties nightclub, Madonna's *Blonde Ambition* is a Broadway musical in all essentials except for its lack of plot.
Charles Shaar Murray, Daily Telegraph, *1990*

Descending a huge flight of stairs to the music of *Express Yourself*, this sex goddess of the Nineties went through 18 numbers and at least half as many changes of scene and costume. The whole show is like a glorified series of videos with Madonna a many-sided vision of sexuality, a pop icon at 31 who revives memory of her start in Lingerie Rock with lace brassieres and flaunted navels but also establishes a new image in the style of a 1930s Hollywood star.
W. J. Weatherby on the Blonde Ambition tour at Nassau Coliseum, Long Island, New York, The Guardian, *1990*

I tried to make the show accommodate my own short attention span.
Madonna

Defiantly steering their career towards a mass market of screaming young girls, George and Andrew pranced around onstage in shorts, their tanned, hairy thighs glinting in the blinking stage-lights, playing a game of badminton that reached its climax when they shoved shuttlecocks down their shorts.
Tony Parsons on early Wham! tour

Some of the best musical trips we ever took were in clubs. Concerts are great but it gets into a crowd phenomenon that really hasn't much to do with music. In a club there's a different atmosphere. They can see you sweat and you can see them. And there's much less bullshit. In a concert situation, you can't really lose.
Jim Morrison

I don't believe in tomorrows. You may be *dead*, but you just
don't know. You make your record like it's the last record you'll
ever make. You go out and play at night – I don't think, 'If
I don't play good tonight at least I played good *last* night.'
It's like there are no tomorrows or yesterdays. There's only right
now.
Bruce Springsteen, *1981*

When we first started playing, I'd go into every show expecting nobody
to come, and I'd go onstage expecting nobody to give me anything for
free. And that's the way you have to play. If you don't play like that,
pack your guitar up, throw it in a trash can and go home, fix televisions
or some other line of work, ya know?
Bruce Springsteen, *1981*

My favourite moments onstage are of silence, when The Police stop
playing. There's just this great blank for the audience to fill in. I often
find myself looking out at them and wondering how I got here. I still
don't think I really belong. Sometimes it's a depressing feeling, but
often it's exhilarating.
Sting, *1981*

The audience create the party as much as the band. At gigs I often
spend a lot of time just watching what's going on in the audience,
it can be such a hoot. I think a lot of people who are interested in
music are fed up with this plastic image they're presented with.
Music is for everybody. It isn't just for an élite bunch of good-looking
men or women who think, 'I'm God's gift and now *I'm* up on the
stage.'
Terry Woods, *The Pogues*

There are perfectly sane men and women who will tell you that those
first Rainbow Roxy Music concerts changed their lives; the
presentation, the cleverness, the stylisation, the audience.
Peter York

It's what I'm destined to do. Muddy Waters is still doing it, and he's
65. In the States there's a lotta old guys that are still doing it and I
kinda feel that when I'm that old, as long as I can do it, I guess I will do
it, because it's all I ever did or wanted to do.
Bob Dylan, *1978*

Rod Stewart has an attractive voice and a highly unattractive bottom. In his concert performances he now spends more time wagging the latter than exercising the former, thereby conforming to the established pattern by which popular entertainers fall prey to the delusion that the public loves them for themselves, and not for their work.
Clive James, *1981*

It was only to be expected from a generation of students – for they are the mainstay of The Stone Roses support – which had grown up in times like these. A few passed around joints, one actually rolled with a cigarette filter in place. Tune in, turn on, take care. Wild it wasn't.
Steve Dodd *on The Stone Roses at Alexandra Palace*

Let it be acknowledged: there are very few performers in the world who could dominate a vast audience of 20,000 as he did. Narcissist, freak, dandy, dancer, rocker, God, devil, stripper, sensualist, tease – the women in the audience are not there for the popcorn – Mr Jagger at 38 is still a kind of wild animal. His athleticism, the result of jogging several miles a day, is phenomenal. He has become the Nureyev of rock'n'roll.
John Heilpern *at Madison Square Garden, 1981*

That person I am onstage, I would hate to be him offstage, because it's a very powerful ego-force. At the same time that is what makes certain people what they are. Whether you like it or not, U2 have, for better or worse, filled some kind of quasi-spiritual rock'n'roll void, especially in the States. Now that type of thing has *got* to have an effect on Bono. Sure, he comes across as being incredibly pompous, but people are determined not to see his funny side.
Terence Trent D'Arby, *1989*

It's ridiculous. Some people still see us as a drunken novelty act even after four albums and seven years and Christ knows how many successful tours.
Spider Stacy, *The Pogues, 1989*

One day we had this gig at the arts centre and I had this little old drum machine. At a certain moment we had it going with some echo loops and some feedback and we just left the stage and joined the dancers. It kept on going for an hour or so.
Ralf Hütter, *Kraftwerk, 1987*

It's a toss-up whether Genesis would be better or worse without Phil. True, none of the others can sing, but a Phil-free Genesis would at least rid the proceedings of his ingratiating attempts to be humorous and entertaining. He gets everyone to wave their arms in the air and shout, 'ooh!' He stumps around the stage making thumbs-up signs into the front rows like a pantomime chimney-sweep. Really funny if you like Charlie Drake.
Adam Sweeting on *Genesis at Earls Court, 1992*

An agreeable, if sometimes workaday performer with a safe pair of hands, at 38 Petty may have consigned himself to the old boys' club a bit ahead of his time. But if anyone is capable of carrying the banner of traditional rock'n'roll towards the millennium with grace and humour, it is him.
David Sinclair on *Tom Petty at Wembley Arena, 1992*

Lou wanted respect. It was announced that nobody would be permitted to enter the auditorium during songs, and that petulant Dame Louis would leave the stage if people shouted requests at him. It'll be formal attire next.
Adam Sweeting on *Lou Reed at Hammersmith, 1992*

He's at his best when marching fearlessly into yawning canyons of schlock, epitomised by his all-time end-of-party smoocher *Three Times A Lady*. When Lionel sang it, dozens of couples threw their arms round each other's necks and began to sway clumsily, as if Richie had pressed some biological Go button.
Adam Sweeting on *Lionel Richie at the Town and Country, 1992*

Paul's cleanness and natural sense of showbiz makes the energy of his performance breezily expansive. Unfortunately, this amiably mild kick is delivered in Dachau franchises, to bedraggled and benumbed animals . . . Olympia is like many large concert venues: when fully packed it closely resembles the concentration camp scenes in Wertmuller's *Seven Beauties*. A greyish darkness piled with sullen, lumpy half-dead whelps.
Lester Bangs on *Wings, 1976*

Kilburn and The Waterboys were made for each other, now that Mike Scott and his band of gypsies seem to have adopted Galway as their centre of operations . . . Meanwhile, the entire hall was swaying like the Liverpool ferry in a heavy swell. The Waterboys crowd is a riotous assembly of timewarped punks, stubbly young men of poetic aspect in

loose-fitting shirts and long hair, people clearly familiar with the clubs and pubs where traditional music is played, and others who can only be described as parents. All that was really lacking was a Guinness fountain.
Adam Sweeting, 1989

You don't know what Joe's gonna do, he does mad things, like jumps into the orchestra pit and doesn't reappear for five minutes, but he's still singing down there. Shane would never move from his spot except to get a drink.
Darryl Hunt on guest Pogue Joe Strummer, 1991

The crowds have been brilliant everywhere. The set we're doing now is only half of Shane's songs. The rest is other people's, and versions, and a couple of Joe's songs, and they've loved it, so that's great. It's loosened everybody up more, everybody sings more onstage, and gets more involved. 'Cause when Shane was there it was: 'Let's all do our job. And either Shane will be on form tonight, or he won't be.' The crowd would just stand there watching Shane pouring wine over his head. And he'd play up to it.
Darryl Hunt, 1991

It's quite funny watching audiences' faces, because when Shane was in the group they'd all be looking at him to see if he collapsed, or burnt himself with his cigarette, and occasionally looking at the rest of us. But with Joe onstage they're a bit confused, because they're watching him, but suddenly he's not there for a minute.
Darryl Hunt

Suede's confidence implied that the identity dilemma will be quickly resolved. Their swaggering sense of presence already makes them worth the price of admission. As we left, a girl cried, 'I *touched* him.' You can't buy that sort of credibility.
Caroline Sullivan on Suede at the SW1 Club, 1992

I saw The Rolling Stones in Manchester about three weeks ago. It was fantastic really. They come on, it's broad daylight, the audience is predominantly ordinary people in trainers who look a bit younger than me. You can see terraced houses just behind the stage, where people live, and there's Mick Jagger! And he's wearing clown's trousers, in the worst possible taste, bright yellow, orange and green, and you think What's this? And he does *Start Me Up*. And as the show progresses you realise he's just a master of manipulation. He comes out in those clothes because it's daytime, and as it gets a bit darker, and after they'd done *Ruby Tuesday*, it's dusk and you start to get the full mettle of The Stones. The lights come on and they're into *Gimme Shelter* and suddenly it gets sinister. And he was singing so well! A master showman. Who has there been? Elvis Presley, Rudolf Valentino maybe. And Mick Jagger.

John Butler, *Diesel Park West, 1991*

Madonna

Madonna is the high priestess of pop bimbos.
Tony Parsons

I realise some people regard me as a tart. But I'm just being me. I like
to flaunt myself, it comes naturally.
Madonna, *1992*

It's a great feeling to be powerful. I've been striving for it all my life. I
think that's just the quest of every human being: *power*. There's a
constant struggle for power in a relationship, too – no matter what.
Madonna, *1990*

I'm not interested in anyone I can't compete with. There's got to be
that fight.
Madonna, *1990*

I think I've always behaved as if I were a star. Since I was a kid I have
behaved as if somebody owed me something.
Madonna, *1990*

It was the greatest event in my life, my mother dying. What happened
when I was six years old changed forever how I am. I can't describe in
words the effect it had. That's when the die was cast. I know if I'd had
a mother I would be very different . . . Mothers, I think, teach you
manners and gentleness.
Madonna, *1991*

We're the closest when I'm in a very vulnerable state. The great thing
is that when I am, he's there for me. The rest of the time I roam around
the world like a miniature tank.
Madonna, *1990, on her father*

Madonna is more than a celebrity; she is that perfect hybrid that
personifies the decadently greedy, selfish sexual decade that spawned
her – a corporation in the form of flesh.
Kevin Sessum, *1990*

Madonna is fizzy and dizzy but utterly in control. She is aerobicised to bodily magnificence, but stuffs herself with garbage food, and smokes. She's a baby but a grown-up, a bitch with a heart of gold, a stylised reprobate in see-thru clothes and a crucifix, who pretends to jerk off on stage and says she fears the Lord. She's a feminist who isn't, a conservative who's not. Madonna has an angle on everything.
Dave Hill

I've always had a soft spot for Madonna. It's that mixture of a soft innocent voice and the sexy underwear. I met her once in Los Angeles but she seemed very nervous.
Phil Collins

I'm not embarrassed by nudity. It's beautiful if it's treated the right way. I've always got a kick out of displaying my body. Sex dominates my thinking and approach, and I don't just mean nudity. Those who consider my book objectionable don't have to buy it.
Madonna, *1992*

So I'm not the world's greatest actress. I believe I'm improving all the time.
Madonna, *1992*

The thing about Madonna is that she is the ultimate consumer of pop culture.
Malcolm McLaren

She is driven by a profound sense of unfulfilment. Anyone who exercises ferociously for two hours a day in order to 'purge bad things' is in need of loving care and attention.
Luca Brasi

Bowing to the fury of American religious groups and consumers, Pepsi is writing off its Madonna deal as a multi-million-dollar mistake.
Peter McDonald, London Evening Standard, *1989*

Her singing voice – a squeaky thing of no great natural beauty – has been routinely regarded as a bit of a joke.
Robert Sandall, The Sunday Times, *1989*

At Cannes this year, previously sane journalists fell at her jogging feet just to jot down a phrase from her lips, and a stream of television reporters queued up to be processed through her suite, which had

permanently fixed television cameras, like a jeweller's security system.
Iain Johnstone, The Sunday Times, *1991*

This film is the definitive document on the diva. It tells you all you ever wanted to know about Madonna, and a lot of what you never wanted to know about Madonna. She shows us her breasts, how she performs oral sex, and her mother's grave, where she prostrates herself on the ground with her ear pressed to the grass – presumably to listen for the sound of revolving.
Iain Johnstone, The Sunday Times, *1991*

She doesn't want to *live* off-camera.
Warren Beatty

Life is about the highs and lows, and if you just present the mids, what's the point?
Madonna, *1991*

Yes, I do feel guilty about being rich. It's because of my upbringing. I was raised by a working-class father and we never had any money. I continue to feel guilty about it like I don't deserve to have it, or something, even though I work really hard. I can't help it.
Madonna, *1991*

I'm a very tormented person, I suppose. I have a lot of demons I'm wrestling with. But I want to be happy. I have moments of happiness. I can't say I'm never happy. I'm working towards knowing myself and I'm assuming that will bring me happiness.
Madonna, *1991*

Geffen sent me to a shrink. A woman, of course. It's very helpful. I don't know if going to a shrink cures your loneliness, but it sure helps you understand it.
Madonna, *1990*

I want to do anything I can to promote AIDS education, awareness, prevention – whatever. I think because I am a celebrity, a public person, I have a real responsibility to be a spokesperson. Next to Hitler, AIDS is the worst thing to happen in the 20th century.
Madonna, *1990*

There is a wink behind everything I do.
Madonna, 1990

What Marilyn only artfully suggested and hinted at, Madonna deals with in a no-nonsense style intended to shock.
W. J. Weatherby, 1990

There is Madonna, bound in slinkiest satin, fishnet-clad legs akimbo, comely breasts alluring but dangerously pointed, shoulders muscled like a man's: the belligerent beauty, the sexy warrior, vulnerable yet confident in her exposure, ironic, laughing at herself, playing with her power.
Helen Fielding, The Sunday Times, *1992*

One explanation for the recent outburst of scholarly attention to 'the Madonna phenomenon' is that academics feel a desperate need for relevance, a desire to get closer to the throbbing centre of American life.
Robert Worth, The Guardian, *1992*

The result is *The Madonna Collection*, a collection of academic essays about Madonna that is alternately intriguing and infuriating. It's like watching a group of lecherous monks discuss a porn film in Latin.
Robert Worth

My fame is reliant on the ideas that I present.
Madonna, 1992

Yet it is not clear, despite her assertions of sympathy with homosexuality and various liberal political causes, that Madonna's power and visibility are in service of anything more than her own pleasure. She is therefore perceived alternately as a supremely cynical opportunist and as a cultural heroine.
Robert Worth

Eventually I would like to direct.
Madonna, 1992

I think that anybody that has a business is a control freak. Anybody that is responsible for other people's jobs and is required to run a company is a control freak.
Madonna, 1992

An entertainer is a whole different thing, an entertainer to me doesn't necessarily deal with reality. It's someone who makes you forget. It's like a drug, it's euphoric and I think it has its place in the world. But that's not the only thing I do. I think I'm an educator – and I do think I'm an artist.
Madonna, 1992

I say what I want to say and I feel very lucky to be, on the one hand, a mainstream artist – you know, somebody that has a big influence and a lot of people pay attention. But I don't think my ideas are mainstream and its very unusual for someone that doesn't have mainstream ideas to be as popular as I am.
Madonna, 1992

Whoever I sleep with I'm still a good person.
Madonna, 1992

It's easy to admire the energy that has gone into making this odd construct, half-book, half-accessory. Production values have been skimped on the blotting paper pages, but they've been prodigally spent on the props. The bondage gear! The bikers! The chains! The ropes! The tuxedos! The cruelly sophisticated, extendable cigarette-holders! No moth-eaten, hackneyed bit of iconic paraphernalia has been left out.
John Walsh, The Sunday Times, *on* Mapplethorpe, *an expensive photo book featuring Madonna and friends, 1992*

That ballgown gives it away. In all these self-consciously scandalous scenarios, she's never more than a sexual tourist, posing in the appropriate leathery get-up, with all the engagement of a tripper on Brighton Pier sticking her head into the cardboard cut-out of the fat lady. The palpable fakery finally blows the book's ambitions as a sex manual: the clutchings and gropings are just tentative approximations of sex, like a fashion shoot that's got out of hand.
John Walsh

It's a collection of sexual fantasies in which an astonishing number of pictures are of Madonna *in the act of fantasising*, gazing at nothing, dreamily regarding the mirror, thumb in mouth, finger in knickers.
John Walsh

Now we're under attack by the stupid people, made famous by the stupid media. Time-Warner – the distributors of Madonna, Ice-T and Prince – is our era's undoubted schlockmeister, but they call it art. We

now have a significant media presence in the US that's wholly
dependent on the flow of concocted outrage to keep themselves in
business.
Wall Street Journal, *1992*

Couples

It wasn't even *my* career – it was *Ike's* career. And it was Ike's songs, mostly, and they were always about Ike's life – and *I* had to sing them. I was just his tool.
Tina Turner, I Tina, My Life Story, *1986*

The kids would all run and hide when Ike came home, the man was so mean.
Tina Turner

He was getting older, and thick in the waist; and I know he was worried about his nose – the cocaine was starting to eat through the tissue between his nostrils.
Tina Turner

That was his whole life; he'd beat you and have sex with you and argue and fight, and then go and play his music.
Tina Turner

He'd lock the door, and then you knew you were gonna get it. One night in the studio, he threw boiling hot coffee in my face. Said I wasn't singing the way he wanted, that I wasn't trying.
Tina Turner

He was an evil possessed person. It got to where if I happened to roll away from him in bed at night – because he had to lie in the crook of my arm – and he woke up and noticed, he would start punching me in my sleep! In my sleep!
Tina Turner

His musical fluency was amazing. He could play any instrument – he could walk into the studio and show the drummer what he wanted him to do, then he could walk over to the guitarist and show him exactly the chords he wanted to hear. He had such control in the studio. And I don't know about other women, but that was an instant turn-on for me. I love knowledge in a man, and Phil was a genius.
Ronnie Spector

It was only after Phil and I started making love that I found out just how insecure he really was.
Ronnie Spector

After we'd do our foreplay, he'd get up from the bed and make sure all the lights were out. That way I couldn't watch him when he took his hair off. Then he'd stumble into the bathroom in the dark, so he could rub this acetone solvent all over his head. It was the smelliest stuff in the world, but I guess it was the only thing he could use to get the toupee glue off his scalp.
Ronnie Spector

Going into rehab became my habit, something to break the boredom, like cigarettes. When things got bad at home, I'd get raging drunk, pass out and then spend ten days in rehab.
Ronnie Spector

Thank God I found Alcoholics Anonymous. The time I spent at AA meetings gave me the only sanity I had in the last year of my marriage.
Ronnie Spector

He was constantly arguing. I suppose we had a sort of love-hate relationship.
Chrissie Shrimpton, 1967, on Mick Jagger

His romance with Chrissie Shrimpton, a fragile good-looker and the younger sister of model Jean Shrimpton, broke up early last year. Their relationship endured for four years and was, by all accounts, tempestuous.
Fred Newman, Nova, *1967*

Four years is a pretty long time for an adolescent. Anyway we tried.
Mick Jagger

Mick is so exciting yet at the same time peaceful to be with. We don't have to go anywhere exotic to enjoy life. As a matter of fact, our most pleasant dates have been spent picnicking in his back garden.
Patti D'Arbanville

I wanted to be an actress, and a scholar too. My first move was to get a Rolling Stone as a boyfriend. I slept with three, then decided that the singer was the best bet.
Marianne Faithfull

I remember Mick telling me in horror that John Lennon wouldn't let his wife Cynthia have a nanny to look after their son, Julian. The Stones always thought The Beatles were so provincial. When Mick hired a nanny for Nicholas, he did it as if he'd had servants all his life.
Marianne Faithfull (Nicholas is her son by art dealer John Dunbar)

Mick had me on a pin and he couldn't let me go. He had me on a pin and he was watching me flail and writhe, but it was something that fascinated him as an artist.
Marianne Faithfull

She was with Jagger throughout The Rolling Stones' transition from snarling delinquents to peacock-robed leaders of a new London élite. Mick Jagger, above all, relished his ascent into the salons of families like the Guinnesses and Ormsby-Gores, and the friendship of society legends like Tom Driberg and Lady Diana Cooper.
Philip Norman

Those were the people who were never shocked by us – the Dribergs, the Diana Coopers. They'd seen it all before in the Twenties. 'Cocaine,' they'd say. 'My dear, I was at dinner parties before the war where every silver salt-cellar was *full* of cocaine!'
Marianne Faithfull

I did love Mick very much, and he loved me. But I felt that an era was over and nothing could ever be the same again. Besides, various influential people with The Stones were letting me know I'd become superfluous. The Stones were getting chic, and I wasn't chic enough.
Marianne Faithfull

She was accustomed to the polished young men in the fast-moving trendy set in which she travelled which included Jean Shrimpton and David Bailey. George Harrison was virtually uneducated, graciousness was not his strong point, and he fluctuated between being a know-it-all Liverpool layabout and a sex-crazed youth.
Peter Brown on model Patti Boyd, 1964

George expected Patti to pander to his ego, his sex and his meals. He expected her to learn to be the perfect northern woman; servile, dedicated, available.
Peter Brown, 1964

A Beatle wife is just baggage. There's no pretending any different.
Patti Harrison *to reporters, 1966*

After the spiritual life with George, within a few weeks of going to live
with Eric I seemed to be surrounded by mayhem. I drank like a fish
too.
Patti Harrison, *1985*

Like any northern girl, Maureen ensnared her man the northern way;
by mid-January (1965), she was pregnant. Ringo, like any good
northern man, did what was expected. One morning at three a.m.,
good and drunk at the Ad Lib, he got down on one knee and proposed
to her amidst the good-natured catcalls of his friends.
Peter Brown

I had met Linda in New York, where she was a budding rock
photographer but better known as an ardent groupie.
Peter Brown

On the morning of 12 March 1969 I witnessed Linda Eastman and
Paul McCartney's marriage. Some time the month before Linda had
learned she was pregnant. And just like the two other Beatles before
him, Paul agreed to do the decent thing and make her his wife.
Peter Brown

I didn't blame John or Yoko. I understood their love. I knew there was
no way I could ever fight the unity of mind and body that they had with
each other.
Cynthia Lennon

Wives and girlfriends had never been allowed to intrude into the
hallowed domain of the studio. But John wanted Yoko with him all the
time and everywhere. Before The Beatles had been a band of four, as
close as brothers. Now they were four plus one and it wasn't working
out.
Julia Baird, *Lennon's half-sister, 1988*

Their relationship was, I think, a classic example of mutual
dependency. It was a case where two people really have an enormous
and permanent need for one another. He needed his Aunt Mimi. He
needed that mother surrogate who would be very firm and strong and
dominating, who would really provide him on the one hand with the
protection he craved, and on the other hand with direction. And also

would relieve him of everything he disliked in terms of nuisance, business, responsibility; allow him the sort of free-floating fantasy, a waking-dream sort of life.
Albert Goldman *on John and Yoko*

Double Fantasy is right: a fantasy made for two (with a little cot at the foot of the bed). It sounds like a great life, but unfortunately it makes a lousy record.
Charles Shaar Murray, *1990*

It all stems from Nico actually. She was the one who took me when I was a skinny little naive brat and taught me how to eat pussy and all about the best French wines and German champagnes.
Iggy Pop, *1979*

When we met we were both laying the same bloke.
David Bowie *on Angie, the shorthand/typing student he married in 1970*

The whole world was amazed when Elton got married.
Rod Stewart, *1986*

I lived for a while with one of his wives without realising. Her name was Betty Davis. When I was with The Dominoes I met her at a party and we went off on the road for about six months. I didn't know who the hell she was. She'd get these calls in the middle of the night from him. He gave this interview in the *Melody Maker* at the time saying: White people can't play the blues, especially Eric Clapton.
Eric Clapton, *1991, on Miles Davis*

I was only nine years older than Elvis, and I guess he had to make emotional adjustments when I married his father.
Dee Presley

Seeing her born was like watching Scotland score. It doesn't happen very often and you never get used to it.
Rod Stewart *when Rachel Hunter gave birth to their daughter Renee in 1992*

Bibliography

Many of the quotes were taken from British magazines such as *Q*, *Vox*, *Melody Maker* and *New Musical Express*, from British newspapers, especially *The Guardian*, and from American magazines such as *Creem* and *Rolling Stone*. The following books were particularly useful:

Awopbopaloobop, Alopbamboom, Nik Cohn, Paladin, 1969
The Age of Rock, edited by Jonathan Eisen, Vintage, 1969
The Rock Revolution, Arnold Shaw, Crowell-Collier, 1969
The Rolling Stone Interviews, Straight Arrow, 1971
Twenty Minute Fandangos and Forever Changes, edited by Jonathan Eisen,
    Vintage, 1971
Mystery Train, Greil Marcus, Omnibus, 1977
Arts in Society, edited by Paul Barker, Fontana, 1977
The Book of Rock Quotes, Jonathan Green, Omnibus, 1982
The Love You Make – An Insider's Story Of The Beatles, Peter Brown and
    Steven Gaines, 1983
The Road That Goes On Forever, Philip Norman, Corgi, 1984
Survivor, The Authorized Biography of Eric Clapton, Ray Coleman, Futura,
    1985
Like Punk Never Happened – Culture Club And The New Pop, Dave
    Rimmer, Faber, 1985
Designer Boys, Material Girls, Dave Hill, Blandford, 1986
The Autobiography, Chuck Berry, Faber, 1987
Country – Living Legends And Dying Metaphors In America's Biggest Music,
    Nick Tosches, Secker & Warburg, 1985
Starmakers And Svengalis, Johnny Rogan, Futura, 1988
The Lives Of John Lennon, Albert Goldman, William Morrow, 1988
Bono In His Own Words, Dave Thompson, Omnibus, 1989
A Voice To Sing With, Joan Baez, Arrow, 1989
Bare, George Michael and Tony Parsons, Michael Joseph, 1990
Dylan Behind The Shades, Clinton Heylin, Viking, 1991
Bob Dylan, Performing Artist, Book One 1960-73, Paul Williams, Xanadu,
    1991
Be My Baby, Ronnie Spector, Pan, 1991
Dylan – A Man Called Alias, Richard Williams, Bloomsbury, 1992